EXTREMIST GROUPS

IN AMERICA

SUSAN S. LANG

EXTREMIST GROUPS

IN AMERICA

Franklin Watts 1990
New York London Toronto Sydney

Photographs courtesy of:
UPI/Bettmann Newsphotos: pp. 14, 22, 30, 34, 87, 109;
Culver Pictures: pp. 19, 45; North Carolina State Department of
Resources: p. 43; Woodfin Camp: pp. 47, 85 and 102 (Jim Anderson),
130, 154; AP/Wide World: pp. 51, 60 (Thomas Roff), 71, 79, 90, 123;
Blackstar: pp. 68 (Pauline Lubens), 80 (Paul Miller), 150 (Janet Fries);
Impact Visuals: p. 95 (Ellen Neipris); Paul Efland (Athens
Newspapers Inc.): p. 112.

Library of Congress Cataloging-in-Publication Data

Lang, Susan S.
Extremist groups in America / by Susan S. Lang.
p.   cm.
Includes bibliographical references.
Summary: Examines many of the extremist religious, paramilitary,
and racist groups in America, discussing their hatred of Jews and
blacks, how they recruit new members, and how they may be opposed.
ISBN 0-531-10901-1
1. Minorities—United States—Juvenile literature.   2. Prejudices—
United States—Juvenile literature.   3. Racism—United States—
Juvenile literature.   4. Antisemitism—United States—Juvenile
literature.   5. Social conflict—United States—Juvenile literature.
6. United States—Race relations—Juvenile literature.   7. United
States—Social conditions—1980—Juvenile literature. [1. Prejudices.
2. Racism.   3. Antisemitism.   4. Race relations.] I. Title.
E184.A1L257   1990
305.8'00973—dc20   89-38533   CIP   AC

To my husband Tom, for his unwavering love and support

CONTENTS

EXTREMIST GROUPS

IN AMERICA

CHAPTER ONE

THE UGLY TRUTH

Michael Donald was an ordinary nineteen-year-old kid living in Mobile, Alabama. He was doing well in trade school and played basketball in his free time. On March 20, 1981, he spent a typical evening watching TV with his cousins. Just before midnight, he was walking home when a car pulled over to ask him directions to a nightclub. As Michael approached the car to explain, one of the car's occupants pointed a gun at Michael's head and ordered him to get into the car.

Michael did as he was told. As the driver took the car into the next county, Michael knew from the way the men were talking and acting that they were mean and angry. He begged them not to kill him. As soon as the car pulled over to the side of the road, Michael bolted out as fast as he could and started to run for his life. His two captors chased him and knocked him to the ground. They clubbed Michael's head and body more than one hundred times with a large tree limb until Michael stopped moving. The vicious strangers then knotted a perfect thirteen-loop noose around Michael's neck, kicked him in the face, slit his throat, and hanged him by the neck from a tree.

Michael's body was discovered early the next morning. As twenty-five policemen gathered evidence around Michael's hanging body, Bennie Jack Hays, age sixty-four, stood on a porch across the street with other members of the United Klans of America, reportedly the most violent sect of the Ku Klux Klan.

"A pretty sight," Hays reportedly commented. "That's gonna look good on the news. Gonna look good for the Klan."[1]

Why would total strangers kidnap a young man and kill him so savagely? "It was nothing personal,"[2] the killers admitted several years later. "We didn't know him. We just wanted to show Klan strength in Alabama."[3] Michael was black; his murderers, Hays's twenty-six-year-old son Henry and his seventeen-year-old pal, James (Tiger) Knowles, were white. They were angry that the trial of a black man who had allegedly killed a white police officer in Birmingham didn't seem to be going their way. The white men, members of the Ku Klux Klan, wanted revenge, and Michael just happened to be walking by.[4]

Alan Berg was a Jewish, outspoken, acid-tongued radio talk-show host in Denver, Colorado. On his show, he'd dare anyone in the audience who hated Jews or blacks to call in and tell him about it.

"Are there any Nazis out there?" he'd ask. "I'm a Jew and I'd like to talk to them."[5]

When people called to spew their hate-mongering rhetoric, Berg would laugh at them, then goad them on. They'd rant that blacks, Jews, Asians, Hispanics, or other minorities were the basic problem with this country. That it was their fault that people were losing their jobs, their farms, or their homes. They'd scream about how a Jewish conspiracy in the government was sapping the moral and economic strength of the nation. Some callers warned about imminent disaster. There were signs of it everywhere; soon there'd be a nuclear war in which God would cleanse the country of all minorities.

"You're a jerk," Berg would comment disgustedly, or "That, my friend, is right out of the Looney Tunes."[6] He'd poke a little more fun, belittle the caller, and then often hang up abruptly. The audience loved it, and Berg's popularity soared while the callers seethed with hate.

On the warm early summer evening of June 18, 1984, Berg drove up to his Denver town house. As he stepped out of his Volkswagen Beetle, fumbling for his keys while trying to balance a lit cigarette and a paper bag filled with canned dog food, Berg was gunned down by an illegal, silenced automatic machine gun called an Ingram MAC 10 that could send a bullet through a cement wall.

Although the murderer fired thirteen shots, Berg's body endured thirty-four wounds as some of Berg's own shattered bones and the .45 caliber slugs bounced around his body.

"He didn't make a sound. He just went down like I pulled the rug out from under him,"[7] later bragged one of his murderers, a man who had never met Berg.

Berg had been hunted and then slaughtered because he was a Jew, had an aggressive personality, and was a powerful media maverick. His cold-blooded

This array of weapons was seized during the arrest of a leader of a violent neo-Nazi group. The man was thought to be the alleged triggerman in the slaying of Denver talk-show host Alan Berg.

murderers were members of a militant, extreme right-wing, white supremacist group called The Order.

←   →

Stomping through dozens of cities in twenty-one states, gangs of teenagers with shaved heads, heavy combat boots, and Nazi or satanic tattoos terrorize innocent citizens with menacing snarls of hate distorting their faces. Baseball bats, pipes, axes, or knives are clutched in their fists. These so-called skinheads don't care whether or not the people they hurt are good, kind, or generous, or the beloved children or parents of others. They're obsessed instead with the color of skin, hating people who aren't pure whites. They storm around cities looking for something vicious and violent to do about it.

In December 1987 in Clearwater, Florida, two skinheads noticed a transient man named Isaiah Walker, age forty-one, asleep on the balcony of the Tampa Museum of Art. He was black, and they were mean, so skinhead Dean McKee, age sixteen, and his brother Scott, eighteen, beat him and kicked him in the head with their steel-toed combat boots. For good measure, Dean thrust a knife deep into Isaiah's heart, mortally wounding him.

In March 1988 in San Jose, California, Scott Vollmer, a twenty-four-year-old local white musician, brought a black man to an all-white party. Michael Elrod, a nineteen-year-old skinhead whose middle name is listed as "Skin" on his driver's license, didn't like seeing the black man talk to a white woman at the party, so he lashed out with racial slurs.

When Vollmer told Elrod to back off, the skinhead turned to Vollmer and rammed his knife deep and fatally into Vollmer's stomach.[8]

And in November 1988, a trio of skinheads in Portland, Oregon, spotted Mulugeta Seraw, a twenty-eight-year-old Ethiopian shuttle-bus driver who had just been dropped off at his apartment by friends. The skinheads jumped out of their car, shouted racial obscenities at the man, and then bashed his brains in with a baseball bat. Seraw died eight hours later.

CHAPTER TWO

RACISM AND EXTREMISM IN THE PAST

Why do some people hate other people because of the color of their skin or the way they worship God? Why do some people taunt and brutalize total strangers who merely belong to a minority group and who have done nothing to hurt them? What causes such violent racism?

Racism Throughout History. Hatred and cruelty based on differences—different skin colors, different religions, or different political beliefs—are nothing new. The Bible is full of conflicts arising between different groups: hostility toward Jews is described as early as 586 B.C.;[1] and in Ancient Rome, despised Christians were fed to lions for spectator sport. By the fourth century, Jews were blamed for Christ's death as well as for any other crimes that could be pinned on them.

Even the history of this nation, the freest and longest-living democracy in the world, is riddled with blind hate and violence against minorities. People of various religions and cultures have frequently been exploited, dominated, hunted, enslaved, or butchered. Many of our earliest settlers fled from Europe because they were persecuted for their religious or political beliefs. Once they got here, however, they themselves became intolerant of outsiders.

The Puritans, for example, arrived in 1620 to escape religious corruption in England. Once here, their theocracy—government based on religion—refused to tolerate anyone who argued against their views. In 1635, Roger Williams was called a radical because he objected to laws telling him how to observe God. When the Puritans banished him from the Massachusetts Bay Colony, Williams founded Rhode Island, where he established a freer government based on tolerance for all—except for Roman Catholics. Catholics had to flee to Maryland, where they were welcome, but then *they* excluded other faiths.

Early on, Catholics were victims of loathing and disdain in a mostly Protestant America. When thousands of Catholics immigrated to the United States in the 1830s, they were resented because they competed for the same jobs as those already here. Catholic immigrants were attacked on the street, and their homes were stoned. Later, Catholic churches and homes were stormed and burned by rioting mobs, and dozens of people were killed.

In the 1840s, an anti-alien and anti-Catholic secret society was formed. The so-called Know Nothings provoked riots, terror, and national suspicion against Catholic Irish-Americans for almost twenty years.

Instances of hatred and prejudice against many
different groups are found throughout our
nation's history. In the 1840s, a group called
the Know Nothings was formed; they believed that
Irish and German immigrants "stole" American
elections and were running big city governments.

By the time of the Civil War, many whites had already joined secret terrorist groups to hurt or even lynch Southern whites who were thought to oppose slavery or secession from the Union. When the war shattered the South's economy and ravaged its land, the Southern states were forced to accept Congress-imposed rule by Northern generals. Hard times hit almost every Southerner, no matter how wealthy or powerful the person had been before the war. Although the causes of the embittered South's anguish and frustration were complex, Southerners blamed the now-freed blacks for their misery.

In 1866, just after the war, a secret club named themselves the Ku Klux Klan and vowed to assert what they claimed was the superiority of the Southern white man. Its brand of fanatical racism quickly inspired intimidating night rides and cross-burnings throughout the South. Author Jules Archer, in *The Extremists: Gadflies of American Society*, says:

> *Klansmen spread terror among Negroes to keep them from claiming their new rights. Wearing long white robes, masks and pointed hoods, they flogged, beat and murdered Negroes. . . . Depicting themselves as gallant "knights" defending the purity of white womanhood, they sought to re-establish white supremacy.*[2]

Ever since, the Ku Klux Klan has been stalking, intimidating, hanging, and hurting blacks and other minorities. Many of today's extremists stem from these "knights" of white terror.

Blacks and Catholics, however, haven't been the

only victims of American racism. As the West was "civilized," Native Americans were scorned and slaughtered; their honor, life-style, land, and food were plundered. And the Chinese, who had come to the United States with high hopes for bright economic opportunities, were quickly disillusioned. Instead of opportunities, they faced the hostility and disgust of American whites and were paid poor wages to build the railroads that so vastly improved the life-styles of those American whites.

By the early 1900s, it was the Jews' turn to be victimized. Automobile baron Henry Ford helped fuel an already festering anti-Semitism by publishing lies that the Jewish people were part of a conspiracy to control the world and that they were to blame for World War I. Then it was the American-Japanese's turn. Historian Richard Curry tells what happened during World War II, just after Pearl Harbor:

> *The government committed the worst single mass violation of civil liberties in American history. Yielding to racist pressures and war hysteria, the authorities forcibly removed all persons of Japanese ancestry from their homes . . . and "relocated" them . . . they were herded together in barbed wire stockades and subjected to indignities of the worst sort. Ultimately, they were removed to concentration camps.*[3]

In 1988, more than forty years later, the U.S. government finally approved reparations to the families of the interned American-Japanese (although as of 1989 they still had not been paid).

The owner of this barbershop in Kent, Washington, expresses a commonly held sentiment found during World War II. At the beginning of the war, large numbers of Japanese were evacuated from this city near Seattle.

Vile and vicious acts against people who are different have been committed for thousands of years and, unfortunately, Americans have proved no different than anyone else.

What Are Racism, Prejudice, Stereotyping, and Discrimination? Racism is the belief that one or more races are superior to others. Prejudice is prejudging others. Gordon Allport, a professor emeritus of psychology at Harvard University and an expert in prejudice, defines prejudice as . . .

> *[a] hostile attitude toward a person who belongs to a group, simply because he belongs to that group, and is therefore presumed to have the objectionable qualities ascribed to the group.*[4]

The most common way that prejudice works is by stereotyping people, that is, putting everyone from the same ethnic group together and assuming they all have the same negative characteristics or behave in the same objectionable way.

Stereotypes and prejudice apply not only to race or color but also to any minority. People typically stereotype others because of their differing religions, political beliefs, or cultures. But discrimination doesn't end there. Prejudice can also be based on sex, age, education, or socioeconomic status. And it can get even more petty. It can lie with a group's accent, food habits, names, dress, even mannerisms. All these cases have one thing in common: the belief that there's a superior "in-group" that excludes an inferior "out-group." Prejudiced individuals, for example, may not give a particular person a job simply because they make negative associations with that person's sex, nationality, religion, age, accent, and so on.

How does such discrimination lead to blind violence against minorities? When some people feel threatened and unhappy, it seems easiest to blame someone else for their misery and anxiety. Immigrants and minorities have always been easy targets or scapegoats. Through the years and even today, many Americans believe that minorities threaten their jobs, their homes, their racial purity.

Ironically, all Americans, with the exception of Native Americans, are descendants of immigrants. America has always held its doors open to refugees from all over the world. As President John F. Kennedy said, "America is a nation of immigrants." Even our Founding Fathers were immigrants. Nevertheless, established Americans often don't want the recent immigrants to get a good job, a cozy home. They fear that there's not enough of all that to go around, and if the Jews or the Vietnamese refugees or others get that good job at the bank, that's one less job for them and their kind. In *American Racism: Exploration of the Nature of Prejudice*, authors Roger Daniels and Harry Kitano write:

> *The built-up feeling of what is considered one's own territory, of what are considered one's rights and prerogatives as white men— can lead to a defensive position that results in extreme solutions. And the reasons for both defensive reactions and extreme solutions are symbolized by remarks such as, "They're taking my job," "They're moving next door to me," . . .*[5]

Such people believe that their lives would be better if minorities were put in their place. They resent ethnic groups, such as Jews or Asians, for buying a nicer home, getting a better job, earning a higher salary. They believe that their own life-styles are threatened, that they have a lot to lose if they "let these people come in and take over."

Prejudice against others is caused by fear and ignorance. People understand their own families and neighbors and know how they do things if they are all from the same culture. However, some people recoil from people who are different. Such ethnocentrism—the belief that one's own group is the best, the only "right" or "normal" one—can cause fear. Such fear can generate hate, which, in turn, can trigger violence.

Some individuals take it upon themselves to protect their own people, their own culture, their own religion. Although such nationalism or patriotism can be a good thing and is the driving force behind any army at war, it can become distorted and twisted to wreak hatred and prejudice against innocent victims.

How the Desire for Change Can Cause Extremism. Whether it's family, community, society, or government, some people like things to stay just the way they are. These people are called "moderates," and they are content with the status quo, the way things are. Many people, though, want some change. Those people, who have new ideas for change, are called "liberals," and on the Line of Change that follows, they fall to the left of the center. Traditionalists who want to preserve the best of the past or to change things back to the way they used to be are called "conservatives"; they fall to the right of the center. Often, liberals are called "left wing" and conservatives "right wing."

Far-Left Extremists   Liberals   Moderates   Conservatives   Far-Right Extremists

Leftists   Rightists

Some people, though, want change, and they want that change *now*. They are not willing to work gradually, by bargaining, negotiating, or reconciling with others to convince other people of their ideas and to make up a majority that can eventually change the system. Instead, they want a lot of change, they want it now, and they are personally willing to risk a great deal to achieve that change. Because they carry things to the extreme, they are called "extremists."

"The extremist does not recognize or accept the legitimacy of dissent and is unwilling to compromise. . . . "[6] says political scientist William Moore. Rather than accepting a pluralistic society—one that consists of different social groups that have a balance of power—extremists are antipluralist. They violate the rules of how change is achieved in a democratic, pluralistic society.

Extremists who want a totally new system are called "radical leftists," "revolutionaries," or "left-wing extremists." Typically, the radical left wants a dramatically altered government structure, more government control over the economy (as in Socialism and Communism), more social welfare programs, antitrust laws, and strong labor unions. If these extremists are violent, they will typically attack officials, police, industrialists, and the military. Sometimes, left-wing extremists or radicals are revolutionaries, members of minority groups such as blacks or Native Americans who not only want more power and equality but also advocate breaking away from the government to form their own. Such groups are called "separatists"—they want a separate state.

Right-wing extremists, on the other hand, don't want a *new* state; they want things the way they *used* to be, before the Jews or blacks or others, for example, came into political power. They usually attack social groups based on racial, ethnic, or religious differences. They typically want as little government regulation as possible. They also want as few social welfare programs as possible, and fewer and less powerful labor unions. Right-wing extremists tend to believe in "rugged individualism"; they'd rather arm themselves, take the law into their own hands as much as possible (this is known as vigilantism), and take care of their own problems rather than have a strong government do it for them. Often, right-wing extremists are from a majority group, such as some whites who don't want immigrants and minorities coming in and changing the country. They are also sometimes members of (or are protected by) the police or the power structure. "Their vigilante activities may thus become a sort of part-time job, lasting a good deal longer than most terrorist careers of the Left."[7] They'd rather that America stay "pure," the way they think it used to be.

Thus, extremists are antipluralistic—they refuse to accept that all social groups have a right to coexist in American society; they tend to use illegitimate methods, such as violence, to achieve their goals; and they do not represent the views of the majority.

Extremism in American History. Extremism is not in itself wrong. In fact, extremism is the driving force behind innovation and creative change. Even democracy and Christianity were once extremist minority views, considered subversive and ludicrous by the majority. Many significant events in American history were caused by those considered extremists at the time. The revolutionaries of 1776, for example, were a small minority fed up with what they believed was oppressive rule by the British crown. These so-called Founding Fathers—primarily wealthy, highly educated colonial aristocrats with too much to lose if the British continued to control and tax them—felt forced to use left-wing tactics to achieve political separatism. They took up arms to overthrow the status quo. The Tories, on the other hand, were the right-wing reactionaries of the times. These colonists, one-third of the total, wanted the Crown of England to maintain its control as it had for 150 years.

Over fifty years later, the abolitionists became the extremists of the day. For more than two centuries, slaves had been the foundation upon which the economic and social structure of the South had rested. When the voice of abolition permeated the South, it was considered radical and dangerous.

To management and government, the labor union movement in the early 1900s was extremist. At that time, there were no laws protecting the wages, workday, or safety of workers. The radical voice of workers demanding better wages and improved working conditions was such a threat to the control, power, and wealth of management that goons were hired to break strikes, to intimidate union members, and even to murder leaders. It is only due to the persistence and perseverance of extremist laborers that today we have minimum wages, laws limiting long working hours, and safety regulations in the workplace.

In the 1960s, the violence and rioting of Southerners resisting racial desegregation and civil rights for blacks were extreme. Peaceful black marchers were stormed; a black church was bombed, killing four children. In reaction, the extreme left black nationalist movement was born: Black Muslims advocated that white men were evil and that blacks should break all contact with them. Another part of the movement, led by Malcolm X, urged blacks to arm themselves in self-defense against racist attacks.

←   →

The Bill of Rights protects the rights of any group to express their ideas:

AMENDMENT I:

FREEDOM OF RELIGION, SPEECH, PRESS,

ASSEMBLY, AND PETITION

Congress shall make no law respecting an establishment of religion or prohibiting the free exercise thereof; or abridging the freedom of speech, or of the press; or the right of the people peaceably to assemble, and to petition the Government for a redress of grievances.

In other words, all Americans have the right to express their ideas, no matter how extreme or hateful. Extremist ideas are to be tolerated in a democratic country; but when those ideas cause a split from the democratic process and turn to violence against others, that extremism has become dangerous.

How Prejudice Leads to Extremism. Although the United States of America is probably the most democratic, the wealthiest, and the freest nation in the

During the civil rights movement in the 1960s, blacks were the targets of violence and terrorism as they demonstrated for equal rights and the desegregation of schools. This bus, carrying a bi-racial integrationist group in Alabama, was burned by a mob of whites.

world, many Americans are not content with their lives and the way things are. As our country has become increasingly technological, complicated, and centralized, the "haves" and "have nots" have become more pronounced. Both the "never-hads" and the "once-hads"[8] feel increasingly ignored and shut out, powerless, and deprived of a piece of the pie that they believe is rightfully theirs. They believe that the political, military, and economic powers that control their lives are way beyond their influence and are, to some extent, the source of their problems. Some citizens view the government as too powerful, yet too ineffectual. They feel alienated from the government and are distrustful of it.

Sociologist David Bouchier, in his book *Radical Citizenship: The New American*, writes:

> *There is a pervasive sense of powerlessness in everyday life and work, and as a consequence of all th[is], there is an anxious search for safe, personal, and individualistic satisfactions that will insulate one against the chaos of public life and the emptiness of private life.*[9]

In addition to powerlessness and alienation, some Americans believe that the criminal justice system is totally inadequate to protect them:

> *The triple-bolted doors, electronic security systems, the places and times which must be avoided, the awareness of empty streets and lobbies, dark corners, loitering youths, the legal or illegal carrying of guns, Mace canisters, or electronic zappers might seem to the outsider more like post-holocaust conditions*

of anarchy than the ordinary routines of a civilized community. Compared with the other Western democracies, the level of crime in the United States is fearful.[10]

As a result, more and more Americans are arming themselves. Vigilantism (where people take the law into their own hands) is on the rise. Powerless people can then become dangerous people. Bouchier also writes:

Powerless people tend to be fascinated by power and to identify with it. The fantasies of power, heroism, revenge, violence, and redemption that have increasingly taken over television and movie screens must be filling some gap in people's lives.[11]

The price we pay to live in a free society is to abide by the rules of that society. If we are frustrated and discontent with those rules, it is our responsibility to work toward changing them. But once people take the law into their own hands, democracy and a free society are threatened.

How Frustration Leads to Hatred. The more frustrated people are with their lives, the more aggressive they become. Even an infant will kick and scream when she doesn't get what she wants. The baby's frustration will be vented through aggression. If the baby feels that her mother is thwarting her from her desire, she will vent that frustration on her parent: the mother is the source of the frustration.

Likewise, when people become frustrated because

they don't have what they think is a good enough job or an adequate income to satisfy their needs and desires, they tend to find some person or some group to blame for their frustration. The resultant anger may turn to aggression toward the person or group perceived to be the source of the frustration. Sometimes, their perception of who is frustrating them is accurate—their boss, their mayor, their parent. Sometimes, though, these angry feelings are displaced, and the anger and the blame are put on "other objects, specifically upon available out-groups."[12] In other words, it's dumped on scapegoats. When raging frustration is combined with racism and prejudice, the frustrated person or group will blame an entire race or nation.

Frustration against an individual will cause anger, but since anger, writes psychologist Allport, is a temporary emotional state, it will pass, perhaps after an argument or even after a fistfight. But when frustration is pitted against an entire group, it causes hatred. Such hatred may be understandable: as, for example, when the Nazis during World War II exterminated more than nine million people, including six million Jews (75 percent of the European Jewish population), thus justifiably arousing hatred from around the world. Often, though, frustrated people end up feeling ready to hate. According to Allport:

The sentiment has little relation to reality, although it may be the product of a long series of bitter disappointments in life. These frustrations become fused into a kind of "free-floating hatred." . . . He must hate something. The real roots of the hatred may baffle him, but he thinks up some convenient victim and some good reason.[13]

Prejudiced people who become haters are always on the lookout for danger; they sense that something or some group is about to threaten their well-being, writes Allport. This constant fear and this anxiety cause feelings of inadequacy and a loss of control. These emotions erode one's self-esteem. Jealousy that others are getting better jobs and guilt that they are not getting the better job may be part of their psychology. Such people have a strong need to blame and feel superior to others. They come to believe that the hated group or person is wholly to blame. It not only gives them an avenue along which to vent their frustration, but it also helps them to rid themselves of any guilt that may linger because of their prejudiced feelings.

Demagogues. These dynamics of powerlessness, alienation, frustration, and anger are at the root of hate and bigotry and may help to explain why some people blindly hate, assault, and murder strangers. These bigots are often goaded into violence by leaders, or

The Nazi extermination of more than six million Jews during World War II arose from the extreme hatred one group of people felt toward another group. These men are liberated inmates of a German concentration camp.

demagogues, who appeal to their vulnerable and fragile states of mind. Throughout history, demagogues have gained power and popularity by appealing to the emotions, passions, and prejudices of others, and they commonly use the same messages of protest and hate. According to the authors of *Prophets of Deceit*, who studied the speeches of many demagogues, the messages are remarkably similar. They are:

You've been cheated.

There is a widespread conspiracy against us.

The conspirators are sexually corrupt, too.

Our present government is corrupt.

Doom is just around the corner.

Capitalism and Communism both threaten us.

We can't trust the foreigners.

Our enemies are low animals.

There is no middle ground.

There must be no polluting of blood (we must remain racially pure).

But with disaster around the corner, what can you do?

The situation is too urgent to permit the luxury of thought.

Everybody is against me (they're trying to shut me up).[14]

Then demagogues describe how wonderful it would be if . . . and prescribe their own course of action, often a violent one. The listeners are assured that they're not to blame, that they are the true patriots, the true nationalists, and that they are superior to others. People who have a great deal to lose are vulnerable to the rhetoric of demagogues, but so are people who have very little to lose. They might already be unemployed, poor, or imprisoned. Poor teenagers living in an inner city, for example, may believe that they have few bright prospects for the future and that they have nothing to lose by trying to create change. Such people are willing to risk a lot because they have so little to lose.

As we shall see, extremist groups today use these same tools of demagoguery to fuel fear and paranoia.

CHAPTER THREE

A SHRINKING, CHANGING KU KLUX KLAN

In the hands of violent men, the Ku Klux Klan has been responsible for some of the worst bloodshed and terrorism in American history. Its weapons have ranged from the whip to dynamite, and down through the years its tactics have included hanging, acid branding, tar-and-feathering, castration, and other forms of mutilation. Its list of victims will never be fully documented because now and in times past many of them were too afraid to report their suffering to the authorities. [1]

*Klanwatch,
Southern Poverty Law Center*

For more than a century, men and women disguised in white robes and tall pointed hoods have stalked the land, hunting down blacks and other minorities to intimidate, terrorize, whip, lynch, and bomb. With hate simmering in their hearts and weapons clenched in their fists, members of the Ku Klux Klan are obsessed with the message burning in their brains: do everything possible to reassert white supremacy and hold down everyone else.

It all began innocently enough in 1866, when six bored Confederate veterans gathered around a fireplace on Christmas Eve in Pulaski, Tennessee. For fun and adventure, they formed what began as a social club. After some brainstorming, the group settled on the name Ku Klux Klan—after the Greek word *kuklos*, which means circle or band. They agreed that the name had a certain ring to it. They embellished their vision with preposterous titles. The leader would be called the Grand Cyclops; his assistant would be the Grand Magi; the host at the door of their meetings would be the Grand Turk; new members would be Ghouls; and messengers would be Night Hawks.

To add some excitement, the original six masqueraded in white sheets one night and stormed on horses through their quiet little town. Their night ride created such a sensation that the club decided to keep the sheets, soon turned into long white robes, as its official uniform; they later added tall pointed hoods and grotesque masks. New members went through elaborate and harrowing initiation exercises with secret ceremonies and solemn vows.

The secret hooded order soon caught the imagination of those neighbors in surrounding towns who felt alienated, victimized, and powerless by Congressional Reconstructionist policies that imposed rule on the unwilling South. As the membership swelled, the hooded night rides soon became the ritual highlight of the gatherings. The gallant "knights" chortled over their frightening effect on the gullible local blacks, who trembled as "ghouls" swept through town. Soon, such intimidation became their mission, attracting even more Southern whites who resented the blacks' new freedoms and thrilled at the thought of scaring them out of town. Soon, the intimidation led to direct threats, cross-burnings, and late-night visits to black homes; then the threats turned to violence.

By 1867, there were enough separate groups to hold a convention, which declared that the fundamental goal of the Klan was the maintenance of the supremacy of the white race in this country. Then called the Invisible Empire of the South, the organization elected its Imperial Wizard, and members were bestowed with majestic titles such as Grand Dragons, Grand Titans, and Grand Giants. Author Jules Archer, in *The Extremists: Gadflies of American Society*, writes:

> *Riding at night with whips, pistol and rope, Klansmen forced Negroes to withdraw from the political life of the South. Flaming crosses, Klan symbols, were planted in the front yards of those they wished to frighten. Anyone interfering with, or exposing, their crimes were murdered. . . . Night rallies of the hooded mobs, visible on hills in the light of huge burning crosses, intensified the climate of terror.*[2]

No one knows how many people trembled at their fury, endured their floggings, or strangled at the end of their ropes. A Congressional investigation in 1868 reported that in just three weeks before election day, 2,000 people had been murdered or flogged in Louisiana; 72 murdered and 126 flogged in Georgia; 18 murdered and 315 flogged in North Carolina;[3] and 109 killed in Alabama.[4] According to the Southern Poverty Law Center:

> *Between 1889 and 1941, 3,811 black people were lynched, for "crimes" such as threatening to sue a white man, attempting to register to vote, joining labor unions, being "disrespectful" to a white man, looking at a white woman, or for no reason at all.*[5]

Through the years since, membership in the Klan has ebbed and soared, depending on the times. According to journalist James Coates, author of *Armed and Dangerous: The Rise of the Survivalist Right*, a Klan leader consulted two publicists in the early 1920s when membership was down. They advised him that

A rare photograph of a Klansman during the Reconstruction. The KKK's long history had its beginnings in the resentment and hatred many white southerners felt after the Civil War.

*The Klan needed somebody else to hate. . . .
It was no longer enough just to target blacks
and appeal to people's patriotism. The Klan
needed other scapegoats. . . . On the advice
of [the publicists], the Klan declared itself
"100 percent American, 100 percent Christian and 100 percent Protestant."*[6]

What that really meant was that the Klan was to
become staunchly anti-black, anti-Jewish, anti-Catholic, as well as anti-Asian, anti-immigrant, anti-
bootlegger, anti-dope, and anti-scandalous sexual
behavior.[7] The strategy worked. By 1921, more than
100,000 people had joined the "Invisible Empire,"
and by 1922, the Klan boasted 1.2 million members.
"No longer was the Klan a regional organization
confined to the South—it had become a national
phenomenon," says historian Milton Meltzer.[8] At its
peak in 1925, membership approached six million
people, and the constituency was strong enough to
vote some Klansmen into public office.

But ineffective Klan public officials, scandals,
growing opposition to Klan tactics, and the Depression
soon whittled down the memberships. Although incidents flared up here and there, Klan membership
didn't mushroom again until the civil rights movement
in the 1950s. By the late 1950s, the major Klan
network was rooted in nine Southern states, and
almost two dozen smaller Klan units competed with
them, sparking violence. "As the rival Klan groups
sought to outdo one another in demonstrations of
militancy, their competition often resulted in violence, and the use of dynamite became the signature
of many of their activities," states the Anti-Defamation
League of B'nai B'rith.[9]

A wave of repression accompanied by lynchings,
shootings, and whippings swept the country
in the early and mid-1920s. Victims of the
Klan were usually blacks, Jews, Catholics,
Mexicans, and other immigrants.

By the end of the 1960s, there were some fifty thousand members united to fight desegregation. Klanwatch, an organization devoted to monitoring Klan activities, reports: "Klan members were involved in much of the racial violence that spread throughout the South, and the fanatic Klan rhetoric inspired others who were not Klan members to participate in the campaign of terror."[10] Since then, membership has dwindled. Many leaders have been sent to prison for their gruesome racist crimes; internal rivalries and competition for leadership have weakened the Klan structure; and public opinion has turned from favor and support to disgust and outrage at Klan tactics.

The Klan Today. Today the Ku Klux Klan has a membership of a meager 5,000–6,500, a slump of between 15 percent and 25 percent since 1984 and the lowest membership in 15 years.[11] But declining memberships don't mean that the hatred, violence, and racism have abated. ". . . as a consequence of the hooded empire's decline, some of the Klan have concluded that their only recourse is to undertake desperate measures, including the formation of small,

Although the KKK's influence has peaked in recent years, it is still an active group preaching hatred and divisiveness. By passing on their credo to their children, KKK members guarantee the organization's future.

underground cells to conduct terrorist activities,"
writes Justin Finger in the July 1985 magazine issue of
USA Today.

Some Klan watchers believe that as membership
falters, the threat of the Klan looms even larger. The
recent burst of federal prosecutions has made Klan
members more cautious and fearful of being watched,
arrested, and prosecuted. As a result, more members
are joining an "underground terrorism," reports Jackie
MacDonald in the *National Catholic Reporter* (March
22, 1985). Many racists who might otherwise be Klan
members have traded in their white robes for military-
like uniforms and camouflage clothing and have joined
neo-Nazi groups (see Chapter Six) and other paramilitary camps.

Splinter Groups. Today's Ku Klux Klan is in transi-
tion. There isn't even a single Klan anymore; it has
fragmented into a rabble of feuding groups, "an
alphabet soup overstocked with K's," says journalist
James Coates in his book, *Armed and Dangerous.*
There are more than a dozen splinter organizations.
The major ones are as follows:

The United Klans of America (UKA), based in Tus-
caloosa, Alabama. Claiming 1,500 members and considered the most violent Klan faction, the UKA is led
by Imperial Wizard Robert Shelton, who strongly
believes in keeping its "klavern" (unit) secret. The
group earned notoriety, however, when nineteen-
year-old Michael Donald was beaten and lynched (see
Chapter One) in 1981. Although two UKA men were
convicted for Michael Donald's murder in 1983, his
mother was determined to prove further that "Michael
did no wrong." With the Southern Poverty Law

Center representing her, Beulah May Donald filed a civil suit against the entire organization, contending that the "killers were . . . carrying out an organizational policy. . . . former Klansmen testified that they had been directed by Klan leaders to harass, intimidate and kill blacks," writes Jesse Kornbluth in the *New York Times Magazine* (November 1, 1987). The all-white jury took only four hours to deliberate before awarding $7 million damages in 1987 to Michael Donald's family.

Since cash was unavailable, Donald's family received the Klan's only significant asset: its deed to the United Klans' national headquarters building that had a market value of $225,000, although it later sold for only $55,000.[12] And in 1989, the man who borrowed the rope to hang Donald was sentenced to life in prison.

These cases helped break up the assets and power of one of the largest factions of the Ku Klux Klan and showed the nation that the Klan had better beware: it would be held responsible for its members' acts of violence.

The Invisible Empire, Knights of the Ku Klux Klan. Previously based in Louisiana and responsible for violent acts during the turbulent civil rights years, this faction is now based in Connecticut and represents the only national Klan with a significant membership outside the South. Its active membership in Connecticut is down to only about fifty members (but 1,500–2,000 nationally), yet Imperial Wizard James Farrands is making a notable effort to link up with other hate groups around the country. In early 1988 at an Invisible Empire rally in Texas, Klansmen were joined by a group of Dallas skinheads. Their goal: "Racial purity—we believe that all civilizations were the result of creativity of the White Race and that the fall of civilization in the past resulted because of the decline of the racial purity of the culture—the WHITE RACE."[13]

The Knights of the Ku Klux Klan has two factions. Don Black, leader of one of the factions, was arrested in 1987 when a mob of Klansmen hurled rocks, bottles, and mud at marching civil rights activists celebrating Martin Luther King, Jr.'s birthday in Forsyth, Georgia. The Southern Poverty Law Center stepped in again, suing the Klan for conspiracy to violate the activists' right of free expression. In November 1988, the court awarded the marchers $950,400 in damages, and another gaping hole was burned into the purses of the Ku Klux Klan.

The other faction, headed by Stanley McCollum, has a membership of some 750 and has been recruiting new members by taking on the appeal of a religious organization (see Chapter Four). He is also strongly allied with the Aryan Nations (see Chapter Five).

In addition, Klan groups are known to exist in Florida, Ohio, Maryland, Missouri, New Jersey, Pennsylvania, California, Texas, Georgia, North Carolina, South Carolina, and New York.

Klan Trends and Strategy. In the 1970s, when many leaders threw in their white sheets and pointed hoods and dressed up instead in three-piece suits, Klan membership rose once again. Articulate, charming, well-dressed spokesmen, such as David Duke, the founder of the Knights of the Ku Klux Klan and then the National Association for the Advancement of White People (NAAWP), helped polish up the Klan's public image. Duke got the Klan "out of the cow

In 1980, former Grand Wizard David Duke left
the Klan to form the National Association for
the Advancement of White People. Now a
representative in the Louisiana state legislature,
Duke has helped the Klan and other extremist
groups clean up "their image." But three-piece
suits and being articulate on television do not
disguise the racist tones of their message.

pasture and into the hotel meeting rooms," called cross-burnings "illuminations," and called himself "National Director" rather than "Imperial Wizard."[14] His calm and softened white supremacist public views, claiming that affirmative action had backfired on whites, were aired on radio and talk shows and attracted thousands of sympathizers.

As the leader of the NAAWP—a "Klan without robes,"[15] which is committed to lobbying for "white rights,"—Duke has called for relocating minorities to specific geographical areas. He has been so successful in polishing his image that he was elected to the 81st District seat in the Louisiana state legislature in February 1989.

But while Duke and other Klan leaders were cleaning up for the public eye, many Klansmen were attending paramilitary training camps behind the scenes. According to the Southern Poverty Law Center:

> *Invisible Empire Imperial Wizard Bill Wilkinson liked to appear in newspaper photos with a sneer on his face and two bodyguards by his side, each holding up submachine guns for the camera. He boasted about the weapons his Invisible Empire members typically brought to rallies, saying "These guns ain't for killing rabbits, they're for wasting people."*[16]

By the late 1970s and early 1980s, Grand Dragon of Texas Louis Beam, a Vietnam veteran, was running at least four paramilitary training camps specializing in guerrilla warfare in Texas, and a white revolutionary army was being trained in North Carolina.

The army was the brainchild of retired Green Beret sergeant Glenn Miller, head of the Confederate Knights of the Ku Klux Klan, later dubbed the White Patriot Party. At his paramilitary training camp, Klansmen shed their white robes for Rambo-style combat boots, machine guns, and camouflage uniforms, thereby attracting a number of young male recruits. Miller's goal, though, was different from the traditional Klan aim of racial segregation. He wanted a well-trained army to go to battle in an all-out white revolution that would establish a Southern white republic by the year 2000. The Southern Poverty Law Center reports that

> [Miller] preached the need to secure the South for a white homeland. He told his followers at one rally, "We're building up a White Christian Army. We're going to get our country back. We hope to keep bloodshed to a minimum, but anyone that gets in the way is going to be sorry."[17]

Miller not only recruited active-duty Marines to help train his corps, but investigators later found that his base had a tremendous cache of stolen military weapons, including dynamite, grenades, plastic explosives, AR-15 rifles, gas masks, lightweight antitank rockets, and more. After being convicted for a series of illegal weapons crimes, Miller went underground and sent a "declaration of war" to the five thousand names on his mailing list, telling them that now was the time for the race war: "White Patriots are now honor-bound and duty-bound to pick up the sword and go to battle against the forces of evil. . . . Let the Blood of our enemies flood the streets, rivers, and fields of the nation."[18] The document went on to order the killing of "race traitors, politicians and judges."[19]

Later, Miller agreed to testify against fellow white supremacists in exchange for having his prison sentence reduced. Now part of the federal witness protection program in which the government gives a witness a new identity if he will testify against other criminals, Miller is serving what will probably be a two-and-one-half-year sentence before going on probation.

Miller's ability to turn a small cadre of Klansmen into a rabid band of trained paramilitaristic soldiers illustrates how such hate movements can swell into a dangerous, fanatical army of racist thugs eager to kill and prepared to die for their cause.

The "new" Klan of today still sees the world in terms of race and ethnicity. Seemingly less militant, more professional, and smoother talking, some leaders have wrapped themselves in the cloak of religion to get their message out (see Chapter Four). Others don suits. But the message still stresses the superiority of the white race, which is being threatened by black crime, affirmative action laws (which assure that minorities are getting equal opportunities for housing and jobs), school integration and busing, welfare reform, immigration laws, and other civil rights policies. And "behind the blacks, lurk the Jews," add today's Klansmen and a host of other right-wing extremist groups. The villainous Jews, they say, have infiltrated the government of the United States and have formed a conspiracy to financially bleed the nation dry and to pass laws that victimize whites and protect blacks. They call the national government in Washington, D.C., ZOG, which stands for Zionist Occupational Government.

The federal government, therefore, is the new target for the KKK and the far right. "Today we see the evil coming out of Washington," says KKK chaplain Thom Robb. "To go out and shoot a Negro is foolish. It's not the Negro in the alley who's responsible for what's wrong in this country. It's the traitors in Washington."[20]

To fortify its weakened structure, the Klan is trying out new approaches and fresh strategies. Some leaders are urging moderation and caution for now, urging members to shed their violent image and to try to be more appealing to the masses, but to get their message out. "We can't take on ZOG militarily now," said Dennis Mayham, the Kansas City Klan leader at a conference in autumn 1988 in rural Arkansas where a National Public Radio reporter taped the speakers, "but we can get the word out."

That word is that ZOG is oppressive, brainwashing the nation, passing laws that prevent whites from fighting back, and that members must work together to eventually overthrow ZOG.

Thom Robb, the self-proclaimed national chaplain of the Knights of the KKK, for example, told the Klan conference to take it easy now and to concentrate on promoting their message. "We are reaching out to people. We're selling a message . . . we have to stop, step back, and look at what is our likability. Do we project the kind of image that people would like or are we somebody they might be ashamed of or they won't like to have around?" He urged those present to reach out, not be isolationists anymore, like the old Klan.

← →

Although the membership rolls are skimpy by historical standards, the Ku Klux Klan remains a threat by continuing to distort public issues, victimize scapegoats, and create a climate of hate and violence. The Southern Poverty Law Center states: "The danger lies not in the length of the membership roll, but in the zeal of the members."[21]

CHAPTER FOUR

THE IDENTITY MOVEMENT: A RELIGION PREACHING HATE

I've got news for you, nigger.
I'm gonna be hunting you.
I've got the Bible in one hand
and a .38 in the other and I
know what to do.[1]

Louis Beam, Grand Dragon
of Texas

Shouting from pulpits in churches while quoting from the Bible, dozens of so-called preachers throughout the nation are using a perverted "religion" to camouflage their gospel of racial bigotry and to allure discontented Christians. They pick and choose bits and pieces of Biblical verses and twist their meanings to fit their own philosophy. While masquerading as good Christians, some of these "reverends" and "pastors" preach a downright racist and radical view that brings out paranoia and prejudice, repeatedly triggering violence in the recent past.

They call themselves the Identity Church or Christian Identity, and local parishes have names such as the Church of Jesus Christ Christian, the Mountain Church, the Cosmotheist Church, the Church of the Creator, the Church of Israel, the New Christian Crusade Church, and the Sword of Christ and Good News, among others.

Using religion to justify hate and violence is nothing new. "Nothing is easier than to twist one's conception of the teachings of religion to fit one's prejudice,"[2] says Gordon Allport, the Harvard psychologist. Identity's brand of "religion" claims that white Anglo-Saxons are the descendants of the Lost Tribes of Israel. They are, therefore, the true "Israelites," and the Bible's "Chosen People." Jesus was not a Jew, they say, but an ancestor of white Northern Europeans (Aryans). Jews, on the other hand, are despised imposters trying to pose as the Chosen People when, in fact, they are actually offspring of Satan and must be destroyed. Jews and all other minorities were God's experiments during Genesis until God created the perfect human, a pure Ayran, on the final day of Creation. The Aryan race, therefore, is naturally the superior one, they say. Non-Aryans are "mud" people, claim Identity leaders. Such beings have no souls and are as low on the spiritual ladder as animals.

Identity preachers blame current social problems from unemployment and the farm crisis to public education's decline and the disintegration of family life on "race mixing" and on the international conspiracy and lies of the Jews. They claim that Jews made up the story of the Holocaust and the murder of six million Jews by Hitler's Nazi Germany to try to get the world's sympathy. Jews have not only infiltrated the national government—ZOG (Zionist Occupational Government)—say Identity leaders, but have seized control of the entire world economy and the international banking system and are, therefore, responsible for the nation's economic woes. As the economic ringleaders, Jews, they claim, are also to blame for imposing the unbearable income tax on the pure whites, "God's chosen people." In addition, Jews, they also claim, have stolen all the gold from Fort Knox, making our currency worthless and income tax meaningless. This thinking has resulted in one subgroup, the Posse Comitatus, which refuses to file income taxes.

Thom Robb of the Knights of the Ku Klux Klan and an Identity minister from Arkansas, wrote to his congregation in 1985:

> The anti-Christ Jews want to kill you and your children in a gigantic genocidal bloodbath. . . . They want to steal the souls and to destroy the minds of your children with their hell-inspired teachings. . . .[3]

By first inciting this kind of paranoia, Identity sermons often wind up warning that the second coming of Jesus is impending, but first, there will be a nuclear holocaust followed by an all-out race war. Cities around the nation will go up in flames, they say, while America's heartland will be cleansed of the "mud" people. Identity believers will be the good people pitted against evil, that is, the Jews, just as the Bible foretold. But underneath the "thin veneer of theology and politics lies a hard coat of racist violence. They

Thom Robb, self-proclaimed chaplain of the
Knights of the KKK and an Identity Movement
minister, is known for his violent rhetoric.
He has called for the execution of gays and
elimination of Jews and other minorities
from the country.

stockpile weapons and issue shrill calls to prepare for battle."[4] Indeed, the pastors typically urge followers to arm themselves, stockpile weapons, train for guerrilla warfare, and amass food supplies. Identity survivalists believe that in so doing, they will endure and rebuild God's kingdom of a pure Aryan or white nation.

The danger of the Identity movement is that it sometimes draws in sincere people who are searching for religious fulfillment and entangles them with hard-core racists who are prepared to act on their hatred. "You can't stop a religious movement the way you can a political one because people believe they are being led by God,"[5] says Klan leader Thom Robb.

Identity strikes a chord in discouraged individuals who are resentful of government control and legislation, and who feel alienated and powerless in their lives. Journalist James Coates says:

> *Because it is a religion with all the traditional trappings, preached by Bible-quoting pastors from pulpits in churches very much like those most Americans grow up in, Identity allows its born-again men and women to practice with suddenly clear consciences the bigotry, hatred and even criminal violence that they had been taught from childhood were sinful.*[6]

The cloak of religion helps rationalize the bigotry and political violence that such preaching incites. In fact, it distorts one's basic values, ends up turning vicious bigotry into a virtue, and makes martyrs of racist leaders who sacrifice themselves to the cause.

Leonard Zeskind of the Atlanta-based Center for Democratic Renewal, a watchdog organization for hate groups, says:

> *The important thing to remember is that Identity is not just another theological cult-type movement but actually represents a springboard from which organized facism springs in the United States. It leads directly to the notion of a racial Armageddon but in and of itself, Identity churches can simply be organized to propagate the theology, to teach it to the children, and to spread the message and create a milieu in which other, more violent groups can organize.*[7]

Fortunately, Identity is not a mainstream philosophy; experts estimate that there are about fifty major leaders and anywhere from seven thousand to twenty-thousand followers. Although its preachings may sound far-fetched, Identity provides a church atmosphere that is familiar to many Americans who never would have dreamed of parading around in the white robes of the Ku Klux Klan or the combat boots and fatigues of the neo-Nazis. They latch onto an idea or two that the "preacher" poses, and then may become drawn into the religion-washed racism. Being a "church" also provides a tax-exempt status for the racist fund raisers.

Although there is no one Identity church, Identity "provides religious unity for differing racist political groups, and it brings religious people into contact with the racist movement,"[8] says Zeskind. By providing a philosophical umbrella, the movement threatens to unite the diverse right-wing extremist groups while luring vulnerable religious individuals who crave someone to blame for their problems.

Some Identity churches remain small local parishes that strive for racial purity but are not militant. Others are biding their time in planning an all-out revolution. Although many of its hard-core militant followers have been imprisoned during the past few years for their violent crimes—including murder, bombings, arson, bank robberies, counterfeiting, holdups of armored cars, shootouts with agents of the FBI— (see Chapter Five)—experts estimate that thousands are still out there:

> *Today, an unknown number . . . live largely clandestine lives, their basement storerooms stocked with food and weaponry to tide them over the coming nuclear holocaust. They wait on farms and ranches and even in many cities for the cleansing war that will make them the heirs to the scorched New Israel that will follow Armageddon. Meanwhile, they wait. . . .*[9]

CHAPTER FIVE

EXTREMISTS OF THE "RELIGIOUS" FAR RIGHT

Hate is our law.
Revenge is our duty.[1]

Richard Butler,
leader of
the Aryan Nations

The Aryan Nations. Far in the northern Rocky Mountains, tucked into the uppermost corner of Idaho's panhandle where the powdered snow is revered by skiers during the winter and where cascading streams yield some of the nation's best brook trout fishing in the spring, rests an idyllic and seemingly peaceful little tourist town called Coeur d'Alene. The breathtaking beauty of this mountain kingdom is complemented by the crisp, sparkling air, the fresh, clean mountain lake, and a sense of peace and tranquility.

But there is a stench just out of town in the neighboring logging hamlet of Hayden Lake. If you go up just north of Coeur d'Alene on Rimrock Road, a gravel route up into the dense pine-wooded hills, you'll spot red, white, and blue banners marking a driveway. Beware! If you follow it farther, the "Whites Only," "No Trespassing," and "Welcome Aryan Warriors" signs and the barbed wire fence should warn you of danger. If you dare go farther, you'll come to a guardhouse and a wooden gate. If it's festival time, pacing guards sporting automatic rifles and Nazi symbols will inspect and interrogate you. If you make it beyond the armed guards, you'll enter a twenty-acre spread, complete with army-style barracks, meeting hall, church, bandstand, a watchtower, and a huge wooden cross.

You have stumbled upon the international headquarters of the Aryan Nations, a far-right pseudo-religious militant organization dedicated to establishing a separate, self-governing all-Aryan kingdom (meaning whites only) in the Pacific Northwest. Its founder and spiritual leader is Richard G. Butler, that is, "Rev." Butler of the Church of Jesus Christ-Christian. A retired aerospace engineer in his early seventies, Butler and his comrades are staunch Identity followers. But you don't necessarily have to believe in the Identity philosophy to attend one of Butler's "annual festivals of hate." You just have to be fanatical in believing that the white race is supreme and be willing to work toward establishing a homeland for whites only.

Every summer, Butler invites an assortment of like-minded people to his mountaintop fortress for the "Aryan Nations World Congress." Although these Rambo-charged conventions of hatemongers attract many Identity followers, they also draw in hard-core Klansmen, young and old neo-Nazis (including the so-called skinheads), and racists from the White Aryan Resistance, the White Student Union, and others from all over the country. Leaders inspire the audience by reminding them that Jews and Jew-lovers who have taken over the national government are the real enemy and the source of their problems. Desegregation, they preach, will lead to "mongrelization" of the Aryan race. Non-Aryans, called subhumans, must be expelled or exterminated, they claim.

The main enemy is "ZOG!" sneered Butler when he explained it all to British journalist Simon Winchester. "The Zionist Occupational Government . . . all those Jew-lovers . . . down in Washington. That's who we're going to fight, and we'll win in the end. The Jews and niggers are ruining this country, and we're going to stop them in their tracks."[2]

Butler's message has fanned the embers of racial hatred. In *The Fiery Cross: The Ku Klux Klan in America*, author Wyn Craig Wade says:

> *By 1986, the Aryan Nations was operating a highly secret, dangerously armed consortium of Klansmen, Nazis, militant survivalists, members of the antitax Posse Comitatus, ex-convicts recruited from prisons, and right-wing religious fanatics . . . members represented the entire socioeconomic spectrum from blue-collar workers to doctors of philosophy. Affiliates of the Aryan Nations were uncovered in North Carolina, Alabama, Georgia, Texas, Pennsylvania, Michigan, and California.*[3]

Butler's bigot barbecues used to offer a full agenda of weapons training and guerrilla warfare tactics work-

shops. These included workshops on how to build homemade detonation devices, how to bomb bridges and railroad tracks, how to set fire to city sewer systems,[4] how to obtain fake IDs, and how to use hideouts and deep cover. In 1987, however, Idaho passed some of the nation's harshest laws against paramilitary training (as have seventeen other states; see Chapter Eleven) and against racial and religious harassment. These new laws have lowered attendance; only several hundred people showed up for the 1986 and 1987 hate holidays, reportedly half the attendance of 1982.

The Anti-Defamation League (ADL) of B'nai B'rith estimates that the Aryan Nations now has a membership of no more than 500, although the white supremacist movement is thought to have all-told some 20,000 members and perhaps as many as 200,000 sympathizers.[5] Membership has dwindled in recent years as a result of massive federal crackdowns that have sent many hard-core fanatics either to prison or underground, or have turned them into government informants who "rollover" on their fellow bigots.[6]

Like the Ku Klux Klan, the Aryan Nations seems to be shrinking in numbers, yet recruitment is active

Taking part in what one would *not* consider a typical "father-son" activity, these members of the Aryan Nations organization attend a convention of white supremacists in Idaho.

among youths and among prisoners (see Chapter Eight), while unions with other white supremacist groups are being forged. Experts warn that as such groups dwindle, the remaining members are often the hardest-core zealots who have become increasingly frustrated and desperate, and, therefore, are even more prone to violence. One such group of the Aryan Nations has already been responsible for a wild spree of violent crimes. The group is called The Order.

The Order. In 1983, a group of men and several women came together from three different organizations: the Aryan Nations; The Covenant, the Sword and the Arm of the Lord; and the organization called The National Alliance (see Chapter Six). They just couldn't wait for eventual establishment of an all-white Kingdom of God, so they formed a secret, vicious arm of the Aryan Nations that went under various names at different times. These included The Order, Bruders Schweigen (German for Silent Brotherhood), the White American Bastion, and the Aryan Resistance Movement. The three dozen or so members were dedicated to terror, violence, and extortion in their effort to overthrow the government. According to an Order member who later testified against the gang:

> *The end goal was the annihilation of the Jews, the Jewish race. A more immediate goal was [to form] a covert organization strong enough to attack the institutions where Jewish power was thought to reside, particularly the media. The plan was to undermine the government and eventually bring it down.*[7]

While membership is shrinking among
some extremist groups, others are
joining forces. A common new alliance is
skinheads (left) with neo-Nazi groups.

The way would then be clear to create an all-white republic, they thought.

Robert J. Mathews, thirty-one, was the leader of this terrorist pack. He encouraged his armed followers to stop complaining and do something about their rage and hatred. Armed with Identity philosophy that would justify their reign of terror and inspired by the thriller novel *The Turner Diaries* (in which a group called the Order commits a chain of violent crimes, including bank robberies and counterfeiting schemes to finance a guerrilla revolution, the bombing of federal buildings and public utilities, and the execution of Jews, blacks, and other minorities while establishing an Aryan Christian paradise), Mathews and his paramilitary-trained and well-armed gang thundered forward in laying the groundwork for the revolution, as described in the novel. According to journalist James Coates:

> *In a single year, this one group of right-wing haters was to strike against society as a whole with what was arguably more bile, more venom and more sheer courage than had been previously observed in a fringe group in all of American history.*[8]

Their activities "electrified the white supremacy movement"[9] and included:

> *Firebombing the "enemy's" churches and community centers*
>
> *Bombing an interstate natural gas pipeline and electrical transmission line*
>
> *Murdering a pawnshop owner while committing an armed robbery*

*Assassinating radio talk-show host Alan Berg
because he was a well-known and outspoken
Jew who ridiculed the far right (see Chapter
One)*

*Murdering a Missouri state trooper and an
Order member who talked too much*

*Holding up at least three armored trucks
(including one with $3.6 million—the largest
robbery ever committed in North America)
and two banks, and stealing more than $4.3
million (of which only $430,000 has been
recovered)*

*Committing other crimes, including counter-
feiting plots, bribery, arson, and criminal
racketeering and conspiracy*

On November 25, 1984, the group signed a "declaration of war" that stated:

*We from this day forward declare that we no
longer consider the regime in Washington to
be a valid and lawful representative of all
Aryans who refuse to submit to the coercion
and subtle tyranny placed upon us. . . . Let
friend and foe alike be made aware. This is
war!*[10]

The document then ordered the execution of federal
agents, the police, congressmen, judges, journalists,
bankers, and informants, and ended, "Let the battle
begin."

But less than two weeks later, more than two
hundred police and federal agents with blackened faces
and camouflage fatigues crept up on The Order's hide-

out in Washington state. Everyone but Mathews eventually surrendered. For thirty-five hours, Mathews fought to the bitter end. He fired some one thousand rounds of ammunition before the FBI dropped an illumination flare from a helicopter, which burned through the house's roof, setting off cases of ammunition, hundreds of grenades, and other explosives stashed in the house. Mathews was burned beyond recognition but rose up as the revered martyr of the cause. Another twenty-four members were sent to prison for twelve to one hundred years.

The Fort Smith Trial of the Ringleaders. Although most of the members of The Order were put behind bars, several white supremacist leaders were still free. In April 1987, a grand jury indicted fourteen white supremacists: nine were charged with "seditious conspiracy" to overthrow the government to establish an Aryan nation, five with conspiring to murder a judge and an FBI agent, and one was charged with both.

Although six of those indicted were already serving prison sentences for related crimes, among those charged were the three—and still free—heavyweight kingpins of the far-right white supremacist movement: Rev. Richard Butler—founder of the Aryan Nations; Louis Beam, former Grand Dragon of the Texas KKK and "ambassador at large" for the Aryan Nations; and Robert Miles, former KKK Grand Dragon and now the leader of the Identity Mountain Church of Jesus Christ the Saviour in Michigan and the "brains" behind the white supremacist movement.

Putting these men behind bars for masterminding The Order's crimes would have most certainly crippled the now-limping white supremacist network, but after a seven-week trial and four days of deliberations, the jury returned a "not guilty" verdict. The jury evidently did not believe critical testimony of a conspiracy by a white supremacist, whose testimony was offered in exchange for reduced charges. When acquitted, Louis Beam gloated: "The Zionist Occupation Government has suffered a terrible blow."[11]

The Posse Comitatus. The Posse Comitatus (Latin for "power of the county") is not only devoted to Identity hate theology but also believes that any authority above the county level is invalid. The basis for this belief is the congressional Posse Comitatus Act from the Civil War era that forbade the federal military from interfering in local problems.

Posse members claim that enemies control the state and federal governments, and they refuse to acknowledge their authority. The federal income tax is not only illegal, they say, but paying that tax is downright sinful. Many Posse believers deny government authority by refusing to pay social security and government loans and by returning their driver's licenses and license plates. Posse Comitatus members also devote much of their energies to flooding the legal system with nuisance lawsuits that they hope will sabotage the judicial system, while arming themselves for the imminent race war.

Every five minutes, a farm family deserts farming; every hour, twelve farm families leave farming, and two rural businesses close down.[12] Such victims of the farm crisis are devastated. Posse members give them a convenient scapegoat: they claim that Jewish bankers loaned all that money for new farm equipment because they were confident that the farmers would eventually have to foreclose. Some people, such as Gordon Kahl, a North Dakota farmer who buckled under economic pressure, traveled through the farm belt "helping" other farmers stave off foreclosure by showing them how to file lawsuits without lawyers to clog up the court system and drag out the foreclosure process.

Many farmers, desperate to save the land that has been in their families for generations, fell prey to the Posse's presentations. "[It's] little wonder that some men and women, choked with rage, guilt, and frustration at the loss of their land, homes, and way of life, were willing to listen . . ."[13] says Syracuse University historian David Bennett. Feeling distressed and deserted by others, they think that the Posse seems to understand and knows how to help. Leonard Zeskind, research director of the Center for Democratic Renewal, says:

> *Most successfully of all, they [the Posse] sell farmers a faulty understanding of legal procedures, and before long, while convincing farmers that they are offering them a simple way out of their legal problems, they have moved to talk of impending Jewish destruction of Western and Christian civilization.*"[14]

When Gordon Kahl was approached by federal marshals in 1983 for probation violations in connection with tax evasion, he used his paramilitary expertise and opened fire. Two marshals were killed and three wounded in the gunfight. It wasn't until four months later that federal agents caught up with Kahl again.

More than forty agents surrounded Kahl's hideout. When the county sheriff came through the door, assuming Kahl would listen to him because he was an authority on the county level, Kahl jumped out from behind the refrigerator and gunned him down. A bloody shootout followed. When a smoke grenade was tossed into a stove flue, it ignited several cases of ammunition. The explosion reduced Kahl to a heap of ashes and delivered to the far right yet another martyr. Police later discovered that the farmhouse was being used as a major weapons stockpile, with more than 100,000 rounds of ammunition stored.

No one knows how many underground Posse Comitatus groups there are in the nation today, as most are members of underground networks. The ADL reports such bands in at least thirteen states; others estimate the central membership at three thousand to ten thousand.[15] Experts believe that Posse members are by and large part of semi-independent survivalist groups that are well-trained and highly armed. Journalist James Coates says:

> *Paranoically secretive—with good reason— and recruited largely by word of mouth, the Posse typically exists as cells made up of seven white males along with their families in a given area who operate independent of any national leadership. But this loosely affiliated con- glomeration of Survivalists appears to be the largest single element of the Survival Right now operating on the American scene.*[16]

About a million stolen dollars are still missing from The Order's heists and is allegedly being used to finance the arming and training of other like-minded "super-patriots."[17] Furthermore, the movement's most influential leaders remain free, and other racist, violent-prone groups continue to thrive, including:

The Covenant, the Sword and the Arm of the Lord (CSA), based on a 224-acre spread near the Arkansas-

Missouri border. CSA is an Identity church, but also a far-right survivalist paramilitary group that was home to more than one hundred followers before a police raid in 1985. Convinced that the United States was headed for economic disaster, famine, rioting, and war, the commune settlement stockpiled weapons, food, and survival gear. Even more alarming than the heap of weapons were the thirty gallons of cyanide (one drop can kill a grown man) the FBI found. The deadly poison was being used to manufacture capsules that authorities believe were destined for an unnamed city's water supply. Federal officials also found that the commune was hiding two Order members wanted by police, implying that the various far-right groups were more tightly knit than was previously believed. "These haters are poised throughout the country to offer shelter, succor [help] and other support to any initiates who work up enough bile and courage to execute the sort of violent attacks against the establishment that Identity preachers equate with virtue,"[18] writes journalist Coates. Many members are now in prison.

The Christian Patriots Defense League (CPDL), headed by retired millionaire John Harrell. CPDL is yet another extreme far-right survivalist and paramilitary group dedicated to helping "patriots" survive the almost certain collapse of the U.S. government and the racial war that will follow. Harrell hosts biannual "freedom festivals" either on his 55-acre Illinois estate, on his 232-acre base in the Missouri Ozarks, or on a paramilitary compound in West Virginia known as the group's survival base. He encourages every family to "have a 12-gauge shotgun, a .22 rifle, and at least 500 rounds of ammunition."[19] His "survival conferences"

John Harrell, head of the Christian Patriots
Defense League, stands in front of his
underground bomb shelter. He is building other
shelters to house his followers, whom he says
he will help survive a coming collapse of the
United States and subsequent racial war.

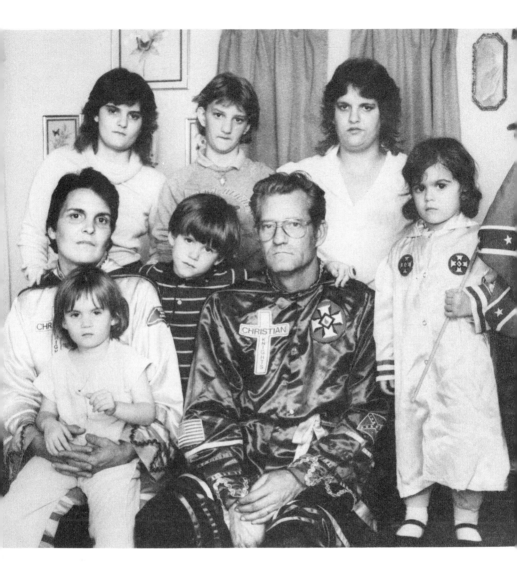

Children imitate their parents. At a very young age, children learn to reject those who are the target of their parents' verbal slurs. As time goes on, this behavior becomes familiar adult bigotry.

used to attract about one thousand participants who had a choice of more than fifty classes related to weapons training and guerrilla warfare before state laws outlawed them. Now attracting some five hundred survivalists, participants are taught tax evasion, first aid, and self-defense to protect the "white Christian civilization."[20]

The Christian Defense League, an extreme anti-Semitic group based in Louisiana that is dedicated to organizing white Christians primarily through its various publications; they are also followers of Identity philosophy.

Journalist James Coates reports of *at least* another half dozen similar pseudoreligious armed survivalist compounds throughout the nation. Because many of these groups are secretive and hide out in compounds off gravel roads in remote areas, there's no way of knowing just how many there are.

Thus, Identity religious philosophy is being used as a way to organize. It's serving as a chain in God's name, dangerously linking together far-right extremist groups and rationalizing their destructive criminal acts. Although scores of these terrorists are now locked away behind prison bars, danger still lurks.

CHAPTER SIX

NASTY NAZIS AND HOTHEADED SKINHEADS

While Klansmen and Identity "preachers" have been spewing their venomous hatred of Jews and blacks to anyone who would listen, another type of bigot has been brewing in the United States: the neo-Nazis.

The neo-Nazis worship Adolf Hitler, Nazi Germany's dictator who was dedicated to "cleansing" Germany of all non-Aryans and establishing a new state (the Third Reich) for "the Master Race" by the 1940s. By blaming their woes on Jews, millions of discontented Germans, vulnerable to Nazi rhetoric in their desperation to improve their lives, rallied to the Nazi cause. When the Nazis took power, Hitler masterminded the horrifying death camps and the "final solution"—the mass murder of more than nine million Jews, Catholics, Slavs, Latins, gypsies, and other non-Aryans—to "purify" Germany.

Although there were Nazi sympathizers in the United States as early as 1933, the American Nazi

Party wasn't officially founded until 1958. Its goal was to rally support for killing Jews and for sending blacks back to Africa. Members wore the Nazi swastika and Nazi-like military uniforms. But this foreign flavor of white supremacy didn't appeal much to the tastes of many Americans; it reeked too strongly of the massacre of millions of innocent men, women, and children.

The Anti-Defamation League (ADL) of B'nai B'rith estimates that there are no more than 400–450 members in the American neo-Nazi movement today, a 50 percent drop since 1978.[1] Neo-Nazism has been so unpopular, in fact, that some neo-Nazis deserted the movement to join the more widely accepted Ku Klux Klan. David Duke, for example, traded in his Nazi swastika to form the Louisiana Ku Klux Klan and, later, the National Association for the Advancement of White People; and Glenn Miller, the ex-Green Beret sergeant who headed the White Patriot Party and the white revolutionary army in North Carolina, also started his career as a neo-Nazi hatemonger. Nevertheless, racial hatred has a tendency to stick around, and the neo-Nazis won't go away. Today there are at least a dozen different Nazi organizations. Some have modified their message and style enough to attract a new breed of followers.

The New Order. The oldest and most organized Nazi group is The New Order, which was formed out of the National Socialist White People's Party, which in turn had been formed from the original American Nazi Party. With its one hundred or so members, The New Order boasts of ties with German Nazis and uses Third Reich symbols from Nazi Germany in its commitment to fulfilling Hitler's mission. The New Order

They're male, female, young, old. They're professionals, laborers, secretaries, farmers. They're found in cities, the suburbs, the countryside. They would be unrecognizable from other Americans but for the bitterness, rage, and hate that fill their lives: they are members of America's extremist groups.

has established a community in New Berlin, Wisconsin, and attempts to recruit new members by distributing fliers calling for "qualified young couples."

The National Alliance. Based on a 346-acre compound in Mill Point, West Virginia, the National Alliance is also strongly anti-Semitic, although it doesn't have ties with Germany or German Nazis. Leader William L. Pierce is the author of *The Turner Diaries*, which he calls the "Handbook for White Victory." It's the adventurous fantasy that inspired members of The Order to rob banks and to print counterfeit money to raise cash to finance a revolution against the U.S. government (see Chapter Five). Recently, Pierce decided to follow the route of the religious right, and he established the "Cosmotheist Community Church," which also gave him tax-exempt status.

White Aryan Resistance. Leader Tom Metzger, a television repairman, was a member of the John Birch Society in the 1960s and the Christian Identity Movement. In the 1970s he joined the Knights of the Ku Klux Klan and worked his way up to become the Grand Dragon of California. In 1983, Metzger formed his own hate club called the White Aryan Resistance (WAR) and he's been busy ever since getting his hate messages out through all kinds of media channels, including his newspaper *WAR*, his cable TV show "Race and Reason," recorded telephone messages, and even computer bulletin boards (see Chapter Eight). His flair for getting on national TV talk shows has made him one of the most recognized racists in the country. He has rewrapped the white power package:

Tom Metzger is one of the more revolutionary
leaders of the white supremacist movement.
He has been the most successful recruiter
of violent neo-Nazi skinheads.

"Where the Old Right was aging, isolated, rural based and mindlessly patriotic, Metzger's New Right would be dynamic, hip, urban, and the champion of a white working class against a treasonous white ruling elite,"[2] said New York writer Jeff Coplon in *Rolling Stone.*

Glistening in its new shiny wrapper, Metzger's new brand of white power not only has a reported following of two thousand adults, but it also has a fresh audience: students belonging to the White Student Union and the reckless, rebellious kids who had already banded together in rat packs: the skinheads.

White Student Union. Dedicated to building "a network of white youth gangs and wolf packs across the nation,"[3] the White Student Union (WSU), also known as the Aryan Youth Movement, is reported to have some thirty chapters in high schools and colleges along the West Coast.[4] Their goal: "Men, women and children, without exception, without appeals, who are of non-Aryan blood shall be terminated or expelled," railed former leader Greg Withrow at the 1986 Aryan Nations conference. But soon after, Withrow had a falling out with the WSU and his old buddy Tom Metzger; he fell in love and then had a radical change of heart. He resigned from the WSU and told TV talk-show hosts and newspaper reporters how Metzger tried to lure teenagers to join up. Not long after, "Withrow was ambushed by former followers in Sacramento and nailed to a 6-foot-long wooden plank. A straight razor was used to slash open his chest," reported *The Oregonian* (December 14, 1987). Withrow survived and identified skinheads as his attackers.

Tom Metzger's son, John, in his early twenties, runs the WSU. He's a chip off the old block:

*Our goal simply put is racial Revolution
. . . we shall continue to mobilize and agitate
on all fronts. We shall continue to encourage
"sporadic incidents" in school campuses and
neighborhoods across America while simul-
taneously rebuilding the hunter-killer in-
stincts in our Youth.*[5] (from a 1988 WSU flier
distributed to schools in Southern California).

In the beginning of 1988, John Metzger had a powwow
with fifty skinheads in southern California. This occa-
sion marked the formal recruitment, training, and
harnessing of the unbridled, menacing behavior of
packs of young people known as the skinheads.

The Youth Corps of Haters: the Skinheads. They're
the Hell's Angels of the 1980s. As young as eleven
years old and usually no older than their early twenties, these mean-spirited punks have formed an unorganized network of violent gangs. Their trademarks
are their shaven heads or closely cropped haircuts,
heavy-duty combat boots (usually with steel toes),
black leather or military jackets, jeans or black Swat
pants, and tattoos of dragons, eagles, "Skinhead," and
satanic symbols. They detest "peace punks," homosexuals, and liberals, but love to rock and roll to the
hard pounding music called "Oi!" that glorifies the
working class. Many also worship similar music, but
with hardline, racist white-power themes.

Many skinheads aren't violence-prone or racist—
they just like the music, clothes, and the street-tough
look. Others stress white pride but don't go around

White supremacist John Metzger,
Tom Metzger's son, being grabbed
by black activist Roy Innis after
Metzger called Innis an "Uncle Tom"
on Geraldo Rivera's television show.

beating up minorities. The most menacing component of this movement, though, is the bands of belligerent bullies with swastikas, death heads, and Iron Crosses tattooed up their arms, down their legs, on their knuckles, and even on their upper lips. Their slogans cry: "Get Out! Jew Pig!"; "Trash 'em! Smash 'em! Make 'em *die!*"; "Make 'em scared! White revolution is the only solution!"

These snarling teenagers are the fastest-growing segment and among the most violent of the neo-Nazi movement—and of the entire white supremacist movement, for that matter. A small cadre of only 300 young people in 1986 has swelled into a vicious, loosely organized army of up to 3,500 teenage thugs in 21 states, scattered all over the country.[6] Some of the gangs with more colorful names include the Reich Skins, the Bashboys (Bay Area Skin Heads), the Death Squad Skins, the Gestapo, and the War Skins in California; the East Side White Pride and Youth of Hitler in Oregon; the Confederate Hammer Heads of Dallas; and Romantic Violence and the Chicago Area Skinheads (CASH) in Illinois.

"This is for real," Leonard Zeskind of the Center for Democratic Renewal told the *Dallas Times Herald* (April 17, 1988). "This is as nasty as we've seen it since the . . . late '70s."

Skinheads have been on a rampage of racist violence, beating and bashing, stabbing and shooting blacks and other minorities around the country. "Skin bullyboys" are reportedly responsible for 1,500 incidents of unprovoked attacks,[7] including committing four murders, defacing synagogues with swastikas, burglarizing homes, and performing other unsavory acts. Their targets include Jews, blacks, Hispanics,

Asians, homosexuals, and even nonracist skinheads. Aryan Youth Movement's vice-president Dave Mazzella calls the skinheads "our front line warriors. They roam the streets and do what's necessary to protect the race."[8]

The Skin Nation in the United States is an imported copycat movement, patterned after the British Skinhead youth subculture that surfaced in the 1960s and 1970s. As angry and alienated working-class teenagers in Great Britain started blaming blacks and immigrants for their unemployment and bleak future, they latched onto the hard-driving "Oi!" music that got its name from the Cockney slang greeting for "Hey!" Many skinheads soon turned to white racist, punk rock bands such as Skrewdriver, Romantic Violence, the Final Solution, War Zone, No Remorse, and Brutal Attack. The rock-for-racism music not only represents working-class unity but also militant pride in being patriotic and pure white. The "White Noise" songs reek of racist messages: Skrewdriver's titles include "Nigger, Nigger," "Race and Nation," and "White Power."

Eventually, the youthful, punk white-racist movement spread to France, West Germany, Belgium, Holland, Sweden, and then to the United States in 1985.[9] In the United States, the bands took on names like the Bootboys, Immoral Discipline, and the Kicker Boys, and their song titles include "Strong Free Nation," "American Heritage," and "I Hate Hippies."[10]

In Britain, most skins are working-class youths, but in the United States, many are middle-class kids from broken homes. Like many adolescents, skins are bored kids who feel estranged from their parents and school. Feeling downtrodden, picked on, and misunderstood, they hang around waiting for something to do, somewhere to belong. Hungry for an identity to cling to and desperate for peer approval, they defiantly join a gang of tough kids, and thus teenage hatemongers are born. As they learn to be meaner and tougher, they start to feel important. According to the *Detroit Free Press* (November 19, 1987):

> *It gives them a target for their anger: Jews, blacks and other minorities, who they believe have robbed them of their rightful, dominant place in the world. It pumps them up with a sense of power they lack. They are transformed from cast-offs into heroes, ready to defend the country from "intruders."* . . .

Although some of these troubled youths outgrow their racist roughneck phase, others will absorb the racist rhetoric that is pounded into them. From a disenchanted youth with nothing to do, the step to becoming a full-fledged fascist is not far off.

"Tom Metzger's hope is that the skinheads will become educated racists like he is and that they'll penetrate into the military, the government, all aspects of life, until they can seize power," Doug Seymour of the Center for Democratic Renewal told *Rolling Stone* (December 1, 1988).

Seventeen-year-old Liz was an A student in Dallas in April 1988, with plans to be a lawyer. She became a skinhead since she couldn't stand punk rockers because they're into drugs and hippie-liberal politics. She thinks that skinheads, on the other hand, are tough and patriotic, and that their close-cropped haircut symbolizes their alienation from the hippie longhairs. "Skinheads aren't afraid to fight for what they believe in," Liz told the *Dallas Times Herald* (April 17, 1988). But don't get her wrong; she doesn't hate blacks. "I just don't want to go to school with them or work with them." Though denying that she's a Nazi, Liz boasts of her white pride. She and her gang also don't believe that the Holocaust, in which nine million people met their deaths, ever took place.

"What makes a Skinhead?" repeated nineteen-year-old Mike of Detroit when asked by Deborah Kaplan, formerly of the *Detroit Free Press*. "Attitude. White power. 'Cause niggers suck. Niggers and Jews. They're half monkeys. They should all be killed."

Or consider the view of Brian, a fifteen-year-old "street warrior" in St. Petersburg, Florida: "We're standing up for our race. I don't care about the Jews. I just want the white race to be pure . . . I want to preach what I believe in." And the thinking of Boris, a teenage skinhead in Tampa, Florida, who wears a silver chain from a pierced hole in his nose to his pierced ear: "I'm a skinhead because I'm proud of my country."[11]

Bob is a twenty-year-old skinhead living in San Francisco. He's got sixteen tattoos, including ones that say "Skins," etched across his chest and inside his lower lip. "We'll take anybody who's into revolution, who's putting his face out, his butt out, his voice out," he told Jeff Coplon of *Rolling Stone*. "When the storm comes, a lot of people will be saying, 'Skinheads, wait for us.' "

One of the meanest skinheads is Clark Martell, who heads the Chicago area skinheads. He was arrested for allegedly breaking into the home of a girl who deserted the skinhead ranks and spraying her face with mace, "beating her limp and painting a

Skinheads represent a new streak of racism. These teenagers are extremely violent and vehement in their hatred of blacks, Jews, Asians, Hispanics, and homosexuals. They are direct and to the point about their goal: white power. These skinheads clashed with anti-Klan demonstrators outside the Democratic National Convention in Atlanta in July 1988.

swastika on the wall with her blood," reported Coplon. "I am a violent person," Martell told Coplon. "I love the white race, and if you love something, you're the most vicious person on earth."

Wherever these street-tough, teenage tyrants have been seen, violence and destruction have followed. "Their record of violence . . . is staggering considering their relatively small numbers,"[12] reports the Center for Democratic Renewal. "There have been skinhead activities in areas where racist activities have never made inroads before," David Lowe, an associate director of ADL, told *Time* magazine (November 28, 1988). "They are young kids, and they are very mobile."

"These are not high school kids out on some lark," said Mark Briskman, the director of the North Texas–Oklahoma office of the ADL. "They are 16- to 20-year-olds who are into Nazi ideology and paraphernalia. It's hard for rational people to understand. They promote bigotry and hatred. Add drugs or alcohol to that and you have a potent combination. Their violence has been demonstrated across the country."[13]

As the numbers of skinheads have increased in the past few years, so has racial violence at a time when the Ku Klux Klan is suffering from a sagging membership. The ADL reported in October 1988 that there was a 17 percent increase in anti-Semitic crime, with a 121 percent increase in California where skinhead populations dominate. Klanwatch estimates that at least half of all violent crimes of a racist or religious nature in 1988 were committed by skinheads.[14]

"Murders, beatings, synagogue vandalism: Skinheads have left their mark in the form of criminal acts, many of them violent, in virtually every community in which they have organized."[15] Some of these senseless crimes have included:

Stabbing to death a forty-one-year-old black transient man in Tampa, Florida, and knifing a white musician who told a skinhead to leave a black alone at a party near San Jose, California (see Chapter One)

Bashing in the brains of an Ethiopian immigrant in Portland, Oregon (see Chapter One)

Slitting the throat of a young Hispanic woman (who survived), trying to run down several Hispanics, spraying Hispanics with a fire extinguisher, attacking a Hispanic couple coming out of a restaurant, and jumping eight Vietnamese, all in and around Los Angeles

Smearing the walls of a Jewish high school in Atlanta, Georgia, with more than fifty swastikas and graffiti, and with slogans such as "The Skins Are Going to Kill U"

Jumping and then deeply slashing the arms, chest, leg, and knee of a twenty-nine-year-old black man in Spokane, Washington[16]

Beating numerous homeless people in Santa Barbara, California

Terrorizing a fifty-four-year-old black female schoolteacher in San Jose, who was trying to walk through a park, by insisting that she pay a "nigger toll" and threatening to string her up a tree

Surrounding the car of a black woman in Portland, Oregon, shouting, "Why don't you die!" spitting on her windshield, and flinging a chain through her window (shattered glass entered her eye)

And the list goes on and on and on.

But if this all isn't frightening enough, consider what would happen if all the mean, nasty white supremacists, young and old, rural and urban, got together and started to cooperate with each other. That's just what has started to happen.

CHAPTER SEVEN

A NEW UNION OF RACISTS

They are farmers, secretaries, factory workers and professionals; they are male and female, young and old. They wear white robes or camouflage, or suits or blue jeans. They live in cities, suburbs and countrysides all across America. They call themselves, among other things, Klansmen, Nazis, nationalists, or racialists, and belong to a wide variety of obscure and frequently changing organizations. They would be indistinguishable from most Americans if it were not for the bitterness that fills their lives and finds its expression in an obsessive hatred for minorities and Jews.

excerpted from
The Ku Klux Klan:
A History of Racism and Violence
published by Klanwatch

By the late 1970s, the Klan and the neo-Nazis began to realize that they could close ranks by putting aside their differences and working together in the name of their common hatred of blacks and Jews, and the fierce belief that the white race is superior. They acted together in 1979, for example, by shooting into a crowd of the Communist Workers Party rallying against the Klan; four men and one woman were slain, and ten others were wounded. In 1983 when the violent small band of racists formed The Order, they came from the ranks of two Identity groups, a neo-Nazi group, and several Klan organizations. And in 1986, various factions marched together in Chicago and again in 1987 in Forsyth, Georgia, attacking civil rights marchers. At the same time, the Aryan Nations was bonding Klansmen with neo-Nazis at its annual hate festivals in Idaho:

> *There has always been a certain amount of linkage among groups which promote bigotry, despite their differences of style and emphasis. With the hate movement reduced to a "hard core" of highly charged activists, the barriers separating Klan, neo-Nazi, and Identity groups have been further removed during the past several years.*[1]

Meanwhile, numerous unorganized gangs of skinheads around the nation were unleashing their violent energy in the name of "white pride," often trying to outdo each other. "Then came a man with a dark vision for a new skinhead destiny who recruited these roving gangs of thugs and misfits as the brown shirts of a rejuvenated white right," reported Jeff Coplon in *Rolling Stone.*

Tom Metzger of the White Aryan Resistance (WAR) recognized the potential of the skinhead movement for the sagging, aging white supremacist movement. His WAR group and his son's White Student Union began to woo skinhead gangs for their violence, anger, and youthful vigor. Metzger pumped up the skinheads with racist rhetoric, giving them a united philosophy, a cause, a backbone of organization, and a "sense of importance." He recruited them as "urban guerrillas in an undeclared war, as morale boosters and headline grabbers and cheap casualties for his larger army," said Coplon in *Rolling Stone*.

In return, the skinheads gave the middle-aged, balding white supremacists a strong arm at rallies, a magnet for publicity, and a wild reckless trigger-happy zeal that promised to renew the slumping spirit of the movement.

A critical link was forged that threatened to fortify the struggling white supremacist movement. No longer were the young skinhead gangs of street punks worlds apart from the "redneck" Southern Klansmen or the camouflage-clad militant neo-Nazis. By 1988, other fronts of the Klan and neo-Nazis vied for the support of the hotheaded skinheads and have been meeting, marching, and scheming together ever since. For example:

In October 1987, thirteen skinheads participated in a cross-burning ceremony with the Klan, and four skinheads became official Klansmen

In January 1988, the Dallas-based Confederate Hammer Skins went to Pulaski, Tennessee, to offer security for a Klan rally

At a celebration honoring Adolf Hitler's birthday, Klansmen and Nazis join to raise a cross. The alliance of various white supremacist groups has given the extremist movement a new dimension.

In February, Dallas skinheads traveled to Arkansas to support the fourteen white supremacists on trial for sedition and conspiracy (see Chapter Five)

In March, they stomped in step with robed Klansmen in Dallas

In May, the skinheads "stood like rocks" alongside Klansmen rallying in Pennsylvania

In June, eighty skinheads from six states attended an Aryan festival in Oklahoma to hear the Oklahoma City Midtown Bootboys; at least twenty unshorn Klansmen and Nazis joined them

In July, Richard Butler of the Aryan Nations warmly welcomed the skinheads from Illinois, Oregon, Nevada, and Utah to his July 1988 Aryan World Congress, which attracted about three hundred white supremacists from all over the nation and Canada. "I want to especially welcome those youths who are called 'Skinheads,' " Butler said in addressing the Congress. "I'm happy to see so many young people here today. . . . One thing they're going to do when they get the proper guidance is clean up the streets"[2]

In August, skinheads from Wisconsin offered support to the Illinois Knights of the KKK at a Chicago rally

While some of the old-time racists fear that the violent-prone youth will renew a wave of government surveillance, Butler has tried to reassure them:

I know that some have said that we don't want the skinheads, they're violent, they're radical. I don't find them that way. I have found that they are young beautiful people who have awoke to the fact that here they are, they're discards of today's society. They have no place to go, no future, nothing to work for.[3]

To help unite the various skinhead groups, Butler has offered his compound in Idaho for their first congress in April 1989. Although an estimated thirty to fifty skinheads showed up, some five hundred anti-racist demonstrators marched for seven miles outside the compound.

By October 1988, the Anti-Defamation League (ADL) of B'nai B'rith reported that skinheads had joined forces with Klan groups from all around the country and had rallied with them in Arkansas, Florida, Georgia, Illinois, Pennsylvania, Tennessee, and Texas:

The KKK, whose ranks have thinned in recent years, regards Skinheads as useful recruits, not only to help fill the void which has been left but also because the appearance of the shaven-headed swastika-bedecked youngsters brings the Klan additional publicity and visibility.[4]

In February 1989, the Southern Poverty Law Center, which tracks the Klan, warned that the alliance of organized racists and skinheads was continuing to strengthen. "Skinheads are giving new life to the white supremacist movement by bringing in young recruits and providing a more contemporary image than older organizations."[5] Though other Klan watchers report that some oldtime racists grumble about the recruitment of skinheads as asking for trouble, there is little doubt that the skinheads are being warmly taken under the wing of the American white supremacist movement. "It remains to be seen what consequences will flow from the embrace,"[6] states the ADL.

Ironically, there's another alliance brewing. Louis Farrakhan, the leader of the Nation of Islam, heads a group of militant blacks who call for a separate black union within the United States. Farrakhan is also fiercely anti-Semitic. (See Chapter Ten.) Although the black leader calls whites "devils," white supremacists have recognized that his anti-Semitism and his goal of establishing an all-black union is similar to theirs. Roger Rosenblatt wrote in *Time* magazine:

> *In spirit, Farrakhan followers are already allied with white American anti-Semitism; Farrakhan deliberately appeals to that. Recently Thomas Metzger, a white supremacist and former leader of the Ku Klux Klan, contributed $100 to Farrakhan's cause in a not-so-odd gesture of alliance. Haters know haters.*[7]

"They are the black counterpart of us,"[8] Thomas Metzger has said.

Even the skinheads have allied with Farrakhan:

> *Las Vegas skinheads, like many of their counterparts, have embraced the views of black separatist leader Louis Farrakhan. The Moslem leader often preaches a mix of anti-*

Semitism and black national separatism that has been criticized as racist. The skinheads speak of "negotiating" with Farrakhan for land rights once their goals are achieved.[9]

Yet another supporter of Farrakhan is the National Front in Britain, a neo-Nazi organization that embraces the British skinhead movement. The National Front has publicly announced that it supports Farrakhan's platform as part of its goal for racial separation in England. "Finally, another longtime supporter of Farrakhan is Libyan leader Col. Muammar Al-Qaddafi, who gave a $5 million interest-free loan to Farrakhan and the Nation of Islam in May 1985."[10]

In the meantime, while white supremacists are reaching out to unlikely partners, they are also doing everything they can to attract new and fresh recruits.

CHAPTER EIGHT

RECRUITING NEW MEMBERS

To get their message out and bring new members in, far-right extremists have learned how to polish their image for the unsuspecting viewer and when to show off their weapons in front of cameras to grab a headline. They know how to appeal to the young as well as to the old, the disgruntled and the distressed, the desperate and the depressed. They have also successfully adopted a multimedia, technologically savvy approach to promote their cause.

Using the Media. Right-wing extremist leaders like David Duke (former Imperial Wizard of the Knights of the Ku Klux Klan and current president of the National Association for the Advancement of White People) and Tom Metzger of the White Aryan Resistance (WAR) are expert at exploiting the media to get their message out. They wear conservative business suits and display soft-spoken manners for TV talk-show hosts and reporters' cameras. Well-dressed and articulate, these hard-core haters are invited onto talk shows time and time again because they are certain to attract controversy, which boosts ratings.

Duke, for example, 6′2″, sandy-haired and trim, has been on more than one hundred TV talk shows. He's a vitamin and exercise advocate who boasts of his one-armed pushups—and he charms his hosts. Sometimes Duke and Metzger tone down their presentations and "come off sounding rather reasonable."[1] They'll talk calmly about how affirmative action, immigration, and busing are backfiring against whites; they may even mention the plight of missing children and drug abuse to arouse sympathetic viewers.

At other times, Klansmen and neo-Nazis on TV get abusive. Several were kicked off the Oprah Winfrey show, and when Geraldo Rivera got his nose broken by skinheads, it made front-page headlines across the country. Even this kind of coverage is okay with the extremists. "So we get condemned by most people," said Robert Miles. "But if one in a thousand says, hey, right on . . . then that's just fine. That's

TV and radio have helped spread the word of racist groups. In Houston, the KKK broadcast white racist programs on the community-access cable channel to "educate" local whites about reverse discrimination.

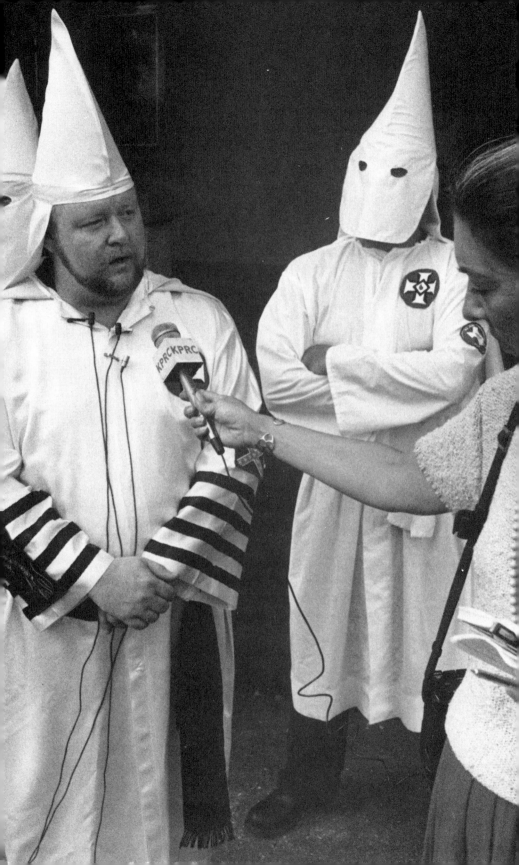

10,000 new supporters for the movement—more money, more noise, more likelihood we'll win. Television is just playing into our hands."[2]

But Metzger has taken TV a step further; he's produced more than forty of his own cable-TV shows called "Race and Reason." They have been shown in at least fifteen cities in a dozen states around the country. Well-dressed in a dark suit, Metzger acts as a talk-show host "interviewing" members of racist groups. "The hate rhetoric on the program is often toned down to give the appearance of a reasoned discussion,"[3] states the Anti-Defamation League (ADL) of B'nai B'rith. There was also the "Aryan Nations Hour" in Salt Lake City, a Saturday-morning call-in show for racists. It was canceled after its host received death threats and a loss of advertisers. The First Amendment, which guarantees all Americans free speech, protects the people on these programs, as does the Federal Cable Act of 1984 that requires local cable stations to provide free "public access" to citizens and prohibits the stations from exercising any "editorial control" over these shows.

This use of "television offers an appearance that racial and religious bigotry has become part of the legitimate marketplace of ideas,"[4] the ADL points out. It also provides a direct line to the more than 100 million cable subscribers. Such free publicity has also been generated by television programs about the hatemongers; the popular TV weekly show "Wise Guy," the HBO special, "Into the Homeland," and the feature films *Betrayed, Mississippi Burning*, and *Talk Radio*, do not portray white supremacists positively, but they do spread the word that such groups actively exist and may strike a chord with certain discontents, who may then attempt to join with like-minded souls.

Computerized Networks of Hate. Right-wing extremists have also been using high-tech methods of linking
up with each other. The "Aryan Nations Liberty
Network" and "Info International," for example, can
be accessed by any home computer with a modem to
get up-to-date hate messages about the movement.
The computer networks not only tend to attract young
computer "hackers," says David Lowe of the ADL but
also can get the message easily over the Canadian
border where some hate literature has been blocked.[5]
Electronic bulletin boards also help incite those who
hook up and spread the names and addresses of "the
enemy." By charging $5 to link up, the computer
networks also help raise money for the cause.

Other Ways the Word Is Getting Out. Right-wing
extremist leaders encourage their followers to take full
advantage of the First Amendment right to free
speech by holding rallies, handing out pamphlets,
getting on public-access TV, even stuffing leaflets into
library books and high school lockers. But their tactics
use other communication systems too, including:

> *home video and audio cassettes available*
> *through mail order*
>
> *telephone "hot lines" around the country to*
> *which "interested parties can call to hear the*
> *latest tape-recorded conspiracy theory played*
> *on an initiate's phone-answering machine."*[6]

Luring Youth. White supremacists realize that the
future of their movement lies with the youth. Adult
racists have organized Klan Youth Corps in almost two
dozen cities. Decked out in racist T-shirts, rings, and

Getting out the word. Klan members hand
out leaflets in Athens, Georgia.

belt buckles, young, impressionable youths are being molded into bigots who organizers hope will grow up mean and strong. "Ku Klux Kids" are encouraged to hand out leaflets in shopping malls and are taught how to become organized in schools along racial lines. They are told to be tough with arrogant nonwhites, to pressure administrators to stop giving in to minorities, to enforce a "tit for tat" school policy (for example, if there's a black cultural class, demand a white cultural class), and to segregate as much as possible.[7] A special Klan camp, now defunct, used to combine racist ideology with sports, recreation, and weapons training (now illegal) in Alabama. "Other Klan efforts have sought to involve children in family-centered social fund-raising activities—cookouts, flea markets, and raffles—that may include pledges of loyalty with Nazi-like salutes and often end with a 'cross-lighting' by adults in Klan ritual garb,"[8] says the ADL.

In North Carolina, for example, a racist group called the Southern National Front, an offspring of the White Patriot Party, went on an eight-town "weekend tour" in 1987, recruiting kids from eight to eighteen. "We're white, we're right, we've just begun to fight!" chanted the racists marching down the main street. After the march, "A dozen or so youths couldn't get enough. They whooped and hollered and pumped fists in the air in the frenzy of adolescent chest-thumping, appearing delighted at saying mean words out loud and in public. They wanted to join."[9]

And in California, Aryan Youth Movement members go after alienated youth:

Leaders of the chapter say they are able to attract five new converts each week because they know their most willing audience: the punkers, the skinheads, and heavy metalists.

The "loners, the kids from the side lawn at school that don't relate to the rich kids in the quad."[10]

Recruiting in Prison. Although many of the most zealous leaders and members of the far right are now in prison, the voices of the movement have not been silenced. The leaders consider prisoners the "ultimate victims of racial or class oppression,"[11] and, therefore, particularly ripe for recruitment. As a result, Robert Miles' Identity Mountain Church, Richard Butler's Aryan Nations, and the Ku Klux Klan have been particularly active and successful in wooing prisoners to the cause. The Aryan Nations, for example, "has been recruiting for some six years now and maintains an active mailing list of some 1,500 inmates," reports *Present Tense* (May–June 1987). It has joined with prison gangs called the Aryan Brotherhood in at least seven states and with the Aryan Warriors in Nevada prisons. By claiming that they are a "church," Identity groups have obtained religious privileges for their prisoners. They're allowed to gather, to have visits from "pastors," and to receive literature.

The recruitment of prisoners is particularly menacing, though, because some prisoners are already deprived and depraved members of society. They are angry at authority, violence-prone, and lawless. With little to do, prisoners have plenty of time to pore over the literature and listen to tapes that tell them who is to blame for their problems. Upon their release, they know that there's a home for them at one of the racist compounds.

One prisoner, Gary Yarbrough, for example, learned of the Aryan Nations while in an Arizona state prison. When released, he went to the Aryan Nations' compound in Idaho, where he became a security guard and then later a member of The Order. His criminal experience was invaluable as the group went on its wild spree of robbing banks and armored cars.

The prison connection not only incites even more racial tension in the nation's prisons but also helps build up the secret army of white racists prepared to live by guns and violence in the coming all-out war against the ZOG, blacks, Jews, and other minorities.

Who Joins? Why do people join such groups? Young people are vulnerable because they're attracted to the Rambo-style tactics, flattered by the attention they get, and satisfied by the sense of importance and belonging. Some prisoners, of course, go for the hard-line racism because they're already down and out and have nothing more to lose. Affiliating with an extremist group also gives them a place to belong, a group to back them up. We've already seen how farmers, desperate to save their family farms, can fall for the sympathetic support of seemingly well-informed Posse Comitatus believers who give them a scapegoat for their misery. Sincere religious individuals, too, can become attracted to the church settings of Identity groups.

Experts point out that people will join such political movements when they sense that their power and status are threatened; in this case, by the affirmative action promised to blacks and by what they believe is the power wielded by Jews. They think that they are the "once-hads" who "represent an economically and socially privileged group who feel that prevailing trends in society threaten them with loss of their position."[12] People also tend to join right-wing extremist groups when they believe that their most basic values are challenged or threatened.

People are also vulnerable to extremists when they feel estranged from their family and peers, or powerless in the giant organizations around them, or alienated by society. They long for identity, acceptance, and reassurance from others. Typically, individuals who join extremist groups are . . .

loners who have few friends. Frequently, their lives are characterized by failure and frustration. They are unhappy with who they are and what they are. They may seek scapegoats to compensate for these feelings of personal failure and frustration.[13]

Writer Pat Jordan in *Life* magazine (November 1986) describes the motley crew that came to the Idaho Aryan Nations retreat:

They come on the run from a bad dream—a failed marriage, a lost job, a bad rap, a criminal charge—on the run from the American dream turned sour. They lick their wounds . . . [and] when the place doesn't heal their wounds, they begin to sulk. Their wounds fester. They grow rabid. In their mind's eye that dream becomes a deceit by their government, by the Jews, the blacks, by the smiling townspeople. . . . A delusion strikes them: We will revolt! . . . A pure race in the purest of lands! An Aryan Mountain Kingdom.

The extremist groups provide a family, a cause, a place to belong, and a way to fight that seething frustration that tears at the fabric of their soul.

CHAPTER NINE

NONVIOLENT RIGHT-WING EXTREMISTS

Not all right-wing extremists stockpile weapons in remote corners of the rural countryside and plan for an impending racial revolution. Several groups work within urban power centers, channeling their hate and prejudice into seemingly legitimate political movements, trying to earn respect and credibility in their pursuit for power and support.

The Liberty Lobby. In 1957, the Liberty Lobby was founded by Willis A. Carto, a Hitler admirer who had previously been working for right-wing organizations and publications. Calling itself "a pressure group for patriotism," the Liberty Lobby, in fact, is "the most active anti-Semitic organization in the country"[1] according to the Anti-Defamation League (ADL) of B'nai B'rith, and Carto is "probably the most influential professional anti-Semite in the United States today."[2]

Now a multimillion-dollar organization based in Washington, D.C., the Liberty Lobby is closely linked with the weekly newspaper, *The Spotlight*. It argues that a conspiracy of Jews and other power-mongers manipulates the government while duping the world about the Holocaust, which the Liberty Lobby claims is a total hoax. Although circulation peaked in 1981 at 300,000, *The Spotlight* has been falling in popularity and now publishes about 113,000 copies a week. The weekly tabloid focuses on anti-Jewish, pro-Nazi themes such as how the white race is becoming an endangered species and how the ADL is "America's Premier Hate Group." Typical articles have also favorably profiled David Duke, the former Imperial Wizard of the Knights of the Ku Klux Klan, and have sympathized with extremist leaders who died for their causes, such as Robert Jay Mathews, who led the terrorist organization The Order, and Posse Comitatus' Gordon Kahl.

In addition to *The Spotlight*, Carto and the Liberty Lobby publish "a wide and shifting network of extremist, racist and anti-Semitic publications."[3] Yet Carto and the Liberty Lobby deny being anti-Semitic or racist and have sued many publications and reporters who have labeled them as such. Nevertheless, Carto testified in a 1985 libel trial with the *National Review* that his views were closely allied with those of Louis Farrakhan, the minister of the Nation of Islam, in that both men believed in racial separation.

To further promote the views of the Liberty Lobby, Carto and his supporters formed a political organization in 1982 called the Populist Party.

The Populist Party. The Populist Party is spearheaded by staff from the Liberty Lobby and *The Spotlight*, "along with a number of KKK leaders and hate group figures."[4] The Center for Democratic Renewal states that the party began "as a coalition of racists and anti-Semites interested in the electoral arena."[5] Although it claims to be an updated version of the populist movement in the late 1800s that represented "the people" (as opposed to the rich and powerful industrialists) and that demanded valid government regulation to guarantee equal opportunity, today's Populist Party is "in reality . . . an effort of organized political extremists and agents of bigotry to cloak themselves in the seeming respectability of nation-wide electoral politics," says the ADL.[6]

The party not only has some members from George Wallace's 1968 anti-integration campaign, says the ADL, but it also has some with "unsavory connections with Klan, neo-Nazi and other hate movements or with armed paramilitary organizations"[7] as well as affiliations with Identity churches and with Posse Comitatus.

The Populist Party advocates the abolition of immigration and the federal income tax, and the dismantling of the Federal Reserve System. While maintaining that it respects racial and cultural diversity, its underlying message is that there should be no tolerance for any minority that divides the majority of the country. The ADL states that other Liberty Lobby literature makes it clear that the "racial minority" that the party is referring to is the Jews.[8]

In 1984, when the Populist Party backed a presidential and vice presidential candidate in 14 states, it received a meager 66,000 votes. In 1986, the party split into two factions, and former Klansman David Duke accepted the 1988 presidential nomination from Carto's faction of the Populist ticket.

Despite all its efforts, though, while "trying to

appeal to a far more educated and sophisticated audience than those small violence-prone groups of racists in the West and South," Syracuse University historian David Bennett concludes that the Liberty Lobby has "made almost no impact in America."[9]

Unlike Carto, though, another far-right politician named Lyndon LaRouche has made an indelible mark on the American political landscape.

Lyndon LaRouche. Lyndon H. LaRouche, Jr., was a left-wing communist in the 1950s and 1960s but made a sharp right turn in his views in the early 1970s. Ex-supporters reported that . . .

> *the switchover resulted from LaRouche's recognition that he was never going to achieve influence within the left; and that on the right, he could gain access to a much larger potential constituency as well as the money of wealthy superpatriots."*[10]

LaRouche soon allied himself with various Klansmen and neo-Nazis, paramilitary training camps, and Willis Carto and the Liberty Lobby. His ideology shifted to a paranoid view of history that blamed Jews, international bankers, and other "enemies of the people" (the same "enemies" that those who are more militant, all-white and far-right also recognize) for much of the evil in the world.

LaRouche's rhetoric became notorious for its bizarre, conspirational nature. A sampling of LaRouche's outrageous views include:

> *Jewish bankers are behind the drug trade, and are peddling their wares with the collu-*

*sion of the royal family of Britain . . . B'nai
B'rith is actively involved in kidnapping
children for fiendish Jewish temple rituals
. . . Walter Mondale is "an agent of influence" of the KGB. . . . The only hope for
mankind is to colonize Mars before nuclear
war eradicates all sentient life on
Earth . . .* [11]

LaRouche blames the problems of the day on Jews
and on what he believes are their centuries-long list of
"crimes" of conspiracy:

*To LaRouche, American Jews are "treason-
ous." . . . [Their] conspiracy is global, La-
Rouche says, operating through a vast network of agents in both Western and communist nations and with a goal of genocide
against the human race—to be achieved via
usury, famine, plague and nuclear war. Unless the conspirators are stopped, LaRouche
predicts, they will succeed in killing more
than two billion people and ushering in a
new Dark Age.* [12]

LaRouche works toward ridding the nation not only
of the Jewish lobby but of "their British agents." La-
Rouche contends that the British are clever, wicked
animals of a nonhuman race that have evolved from
years of inbreeding.

Using deceptively official-sounding names, such
as the "National Democratic Policy Committee"
(which sounds suspiciously like the National Democratic Party), the "National Caucus of Labor Committees," the "U.S. Labor Party," and the "National
Anti-Drug Coalition," LaRouche has managed to at-

tract a number of naive individuals who think that they are joining conservative committees or coalitions that support traditional issues or values when, in fact, they are getting involved in "a fringe political cult practicing extremism that defies categorizing."[13]

To drive his points home, LaRouche not only gets his supporters to peddle his materials at airports, but also "supporters of the movement frequently harass and badger public officials, threaten opponents and defame them with potentially libelous slurs"[14] and have even physically assaulted rivals. LaRouche also has filed many lawsuits for being the victim of libel and slander.

Despite LaRouche's preposterous ideas and his detestable tactics, he managed to raise some $30 million a year by the mid-1980s; to buy a luxurious $4.3 million, 171-acre estate in Leesburg, Virginia; and to back more than two hundred candidates in almost thirty states in the 1986 elections. Although no LaRouche candidates have ever won, "they did pile

There are nonviolent right-wing extremist groups at work in the United States, too. Lyndon LaRouche is one of the better-known personalities in this area. He has supported hundreds of political candidates who espouse his views and has run for public office himself.

up millions of votes and had a profound and surprising impact on national political life, particularly in California and Illinois."[15] In the 1986 Illinois primaries, for example:

> *Democratic voters were startled to find they had nominated a pair of NDPC [National Democratic Policy Committee] to run for the top-level offices of lieutenant governor and secretary of state—bringing the LaRouche party into notoriety . . . [and sending] a political chill across the country."[16]*

Political experts suspect that these successes were due to voter confusion, ignorance, and apathy, although some voters probably voted for the LaRouche candidates because they were attracted to their nonethnic-sounding names. Others say that even some of the candidates may have been confused because LaRouche duped "unsuspecting citizens to run for office under their banner."[17]

LaRouche not only has had candidates nationwide but also has been running for public office himself—since 1976, he has been running for president. Although he has only earned a fraction of the electorate, he was able to muster half a million dollars in matching federal funds in the 1980 and 1984 elections and $100,000 in the 1988 election.

Although experts claim that LaRouche has, at most, only a few thousand hard-core followers, his activities are a threat to the United States:

> *The potential threat to America's democratic values and institutions posed by the LaRouche political cult derives from the*

movement's thriving on secrecy, deception, disruption, fear and hostile confrontations, and its peculiar brand of erratic, bigotry-laced extremism, cunningly camouflaged by the outward respectability of front groups and business suits.[18]

Recently, though, LaRouche and his followers have encountered a major setback. After four years of investigations, LaRouche was convicted of federal conspiracy, mail fraud, tax evasion, and for swindling $30 million from contributors who thought they were lending him money. LaRouche was sentenced in February 1989 to fifteen years in prison. He will be eligible for parole in 1994. Also sentenced were six codefendants who went to prison for three to five years each. LaRouche claims that his sentence is the government's way of eliminating him from the political scene and that his enemies will kill him in prison.

How LaRouche and his followers will operate from prison or rally support after their release remains to be seen.

CHAPTER TEN

THE EXTREME LEFT: LOUIS FARRAKHAN AND OTHERS

Most extremists in the United States today are members of the far right—primarily white supremacists who are racial and religious bigots. Yet several left-wing extremist groups advocate different, though equally radical positions.

As the civil rights movement gained momentum in the late 1950s through the 1960s and was joined by the anti-Vietnam War movement of the late 1960s and early 1970s, left-wing extremism flourished. The diverse groups included the Weather Underground, which was the violent arm of the Students for a Democratic Society (SDS), whose goal was to halt the "imperialism" of the United States, seize power, and create a socialist society; the Black Panthers, which sought cultural nationalism for American blacks; and the Black Liberation Army, a paramilitary group seeking a separate black state. These organizations attracted individuals who were frustrated by government policies and by the slow pace of social change.

After the Vietnam War ended in 1975, the rebellious white youths in some of the extremist groups joined the middle class, and affirmative action regulations that attempted to guarantee equal employment opportunities quelled the militancy of many blacks. Left-wing extremism, for the most part, subsided by the 1980s.

One very vocal left-wing extremist who is still rousing thousands of supporters, though, is a man with racist and anti-Semitic attitudes very similar to those of the far right, except that this man is black.

Louis Farrakhan. Louis Farrakhan began his career in the 1950s as a calypso musician, but left to join Malcolm X, the charismatic spokesman for the Nation of Islam, a black Islamic sect founded in the 1930s by a Southern black farm laborer named Elijah Muhammad. Disillusioned with American Christianity, Muhammad embraced the Islamic religion and called for a separate black nation because he wanted to keep the races segregated, contrary to integration—one of the primary goals of the civil rights movement. Whites, he preached, were "devils"; and since blacks were the original leaders of the world, Muhammad said, it was just a matter of time before they would rule again.

Malcolm X served as a mentor for Farrakhan until 1964, when Malcolm X shed his black supremacy ideology and the goal of a separate black union and left the Islamic organization. He was assassinated several months later in 1965. Farrakhan took his place in the Islamic organization until Elijah Muhammad died in 1975.

When Muhammad's son took over his father's organization, he abandoned his father's antiwhite policies. Farrakhan couldn't tolerate this new ideology, so he broke with the group in 1978 and announced the rebirth of the Nation of Islam in 1981, and named himself its "minister" and leader. He continued to preach that blacks were oppressed by whites and that blacks were the true "chosen people" and should have their own separate state. By the mid-1980s, Farrakhan had amassed a following of some ten thousand black supporters.

When Jesse Jackson announced his candidacy in the presidential campaign of 1984, Farrakhan was one of the first black leaders to offer support. Virtually unknown until the campaign, Farrakhan became a household word when his racial slurs against Jews made headlines nationwide. He called Judaism a "dirty" and "gutter" religion, and Hitler "a great man."[1]

After the campaign, he again attracted attention and thousands of admirers when he gave a series of fiery speeches across the nation that inspired many blacks, yet raised the hackles of Jewish America because of his rampant anti-Semitic message. When covering Farrakhan's speech to a full Madison Square Garden crowd in 1986, the Canadian magazine *MacLean's* reported:

> *The black preacher asked the 25,000-strong crowd, "Who are the enemies of Jesus?" Many raised clenched fists and chanted, "Jews, Jews, Jews!"*[2]

Today Farrakhan is considered "the most controversial black American leader"[3] for his "dual message of self-help and hate. The message of hate predominate[s]."[4]

His self-help ideology calls for a separate black economy in the United States so that blacks may be more economically self-sufficient. With a $5 million

interest-free loan from anti-American Libyan leader Muammar Al-Qaddafi, Farrakhan has founded an organization called POWER—People Organized to Work for Economic Rebirth. The organization is committed to providing ghetto jobs to manufacture household products such as toothpaste and deodorants. "Hundreds of black would-be capitalists have applauded the concept. Even Coretta King, who has characterized Farrakhan's rhetoric as 'extremely harmful,' supports the POWER approach to black economic development."[5]

Farrakhan's message of hate, however, taints his message and insults Jews. To a Washington, D.C., crowd, he said: "I'm not backing down from the Jews because I know their wickedness."[6]

When people think of extremists groups, they almost always think of right-wing white supremacists. But there are individuals like Louis Farrakhan, who advocate different, although just as extreme, views. Farrakhan advocates a separate black state. At a rally at Madison Square Garden in New York City in 1986, Farrakhan drew attention and admiration from some people for a speech tainted with anti-Semitic and racist remarks.

*Jews know their wickedness. . . . Black peo-
ple will not be controlled by Jews. Black
leaders will either come out for us, or get the
hell away from us. Who is your master—God
or Jewish leaders?"*[7]

To a Los Angeles press conference:

*There is no black-Jewish relationship on the
mass level. That's a farce. The kind of relationship we have with Jews I'm interested in
ending is that landlord-tenant relationship,
that we-clean-your-house relationship.*[8]

To a Miami crowd: "I can point to antiblack Jewish
schemes that are used to keep blacks from moving on
up."[9] To a New York Madison Square Garden crowd:
"The Jewish lobby has a stranglehold on the government of the United States."[10] Similar messages were
repeated in his 1988 college campus speaking tour.

Like most demagogues, Farrakhan appeals to the
emotions of his supporters, and millions of blacks
praise his self-help program while minimizing or
ignoring his anti-Semitism, "treating the bigotry as a
minor flaw."[11] During the Reagan administration, the
plight of America's minorities was largely ignored, and
some experts believe that, as a result, many blacks
have turned to Farrakhan in their frustration to make
economic and social headway:

*In this climate of political alienation and race-
baiting, blacks have become more desperate
to find a strategy for getting out of their
deteriorating conditions. Farrakhan has
become an expression of this rage and*

frustration. The repeated efforts by Jewish and middle-class black leaders to discredit him are widely viewed by most blacks as yet another instance of racial and political subordination. [12]

While the momentum of the far right accelerates, Farrakhan is creating a rift between blacks and Jews where there used to be a strong alliance that grew out of the early days of the civil rights movement. "Black anti-Semitism is on the rise,"[13] reports Julius Lester, a black Jewish professor of Jewish studies at the University of Massachusetts. Ironically, Farrakhan's "Jew bashing" can "only promote the interests of the far right,"[14] says black sociologist Marable Manning. If prominent black leaders continue to refuse to openly object to Farrakhan's message, the country may increasingly accept that overt hatred.

"Silence assents to the bigotry," said New York City mayor Ed Koch. "If you don't say something is wrong, then your silence says it is right."[15]

Julius Lester says:

Farrakhan's rabid anti-Semitism is a threat to what little moral fabric America has left. . . . Farrakhan's anti-Semitism is an appeal to the comfort and sloths of hatred; it requires no effort to hate. Farrakhan is subtly but surely creating an atmosphere in America where hatreds of all kinds will be easier to express openly. [16]

When inciting hatred in the hearts of lower- and middle-class blacks, Farrakhan is also forging several alliances with some dangerous friends.

El Rukn. Farrakhan has not only accepted $5 million from Libya, a nation that has repeatedly committed terrorist acts against America, but he has also allied himself with an organization called El Rukn, "one of the biggest and most violent black organized-crime syndicates in the country."[17]

Based in Chicago, El Rukn started as a black street gang in the early 1960s, "shaking down local businesses for protection money."[18] It received some federal grants, bought businesses and real estate, and then peddled drugs. Calling itself the Black P. Stone Nation, and then El Rukn, gang members "commit murder without any qualms; they deal heavily in narcotics, prostitution, and other forms of vice. . . . They have an organization structure as rigid as the crime syndicate,"[19] states a 1980 police report.

While claiming to be a religion, El Rukn—now estimated to have four thousand members with a hard-core group of some fifty individuals—has become increasingly militant and violent and has been terrorizing Chicago for years. Members have been seen repeatedly at Farrakhan's rallies, and Farrakhan has called the black militants "divine warriors" who were "born to settle the score," and "born warriors for true liberation who are waiting for the voice of the Messiah."[20] In other words, Farrakhan has plans to use the urban street gang as soldiers in a future race war.

In 1987, five gang members were convicted of conspiring with Al-Qaddafi, who had reportedly promised them $2.5 million to bomb buildings and planes and to assassinate American officials. Although many of the leaders are now in jail for forty-five years to life sentences and including two on death row, federal officials believe that the gang is still going strong under leadership coming out from prison.

Other Left-Wing Activity. Although only fringe, fragmented organizations, several other left-wing extremist groups still exist.

The New Afrikan People's Organization (NAPO). Committed to building a black separatist state in the deep South, NAPO operates largely from prisons and has affiliations with the Black Liberation Army and other prison left-wing extremist groups. "NAPO is fully committed to the building of a sovereign socialist Black nation—the Republic of New Afrika . . . and seeks to free the land by any means necessary,"[21] says its statement of principles. The group is also reportedly providing paramilitary training to black youths.

Black Guerrilla Family. A coalition of former members of the Black Liberation Army and the Weather Underground, the California prison-based Black Guerrilla Family seeks to organize prison members and unite them with revolutionary groups outside of prison.

African People's Socialist Party (APSP). APSP is a black nationalist, pro-Soviet socialist group based in California prisons. It also seeks to recruit black prisoners. It demands the release of all black prisoners:

> *We believe that all the African men and women who are locked down in U.S. concentration camps commonly known as prisons are there due to decisions, laws, and circumstances which were created by aliens and foreigners for their own benefit and as a means of genocidal colonialist control.*[22]

May 19th Communist Organization. An offshoot of the Weather Underground, the May 19th Communist Organization was responsible for a New Year's Eve bombing in 1982 that maimed three policemen. When members Susan Rosenberg and Tim Blunk were arrested in 1984, police found 780 pounds of explosives and some illegal guns. Rosenberg and Blunk wrote from prison that they were trying to "build clandestine political and military organizations and open up campaigns of armed propaganda against the U.S. military."[23]

John Brown Anti-Klan Committee (JBAKC). Based in New York, JBAKC sounds like a valid organization committed to fighting the Ku Klux Klan, but according to the Anti-Defamation League of B'nai B'rith, it "actually promotes racism and advocates organized violence."[24] With chapters in thirteen states, JBAKC is thought to be a front for the May 19th Communist Organization and also works in collaboration with NAPO. Though fighting Klan activities, it supports "the struggle to free the Black Nation"[25] and also . . .

> *calls for independence for other "oppressed nations" including Mexicans, Puerto Ricans and Native Americans, and it supports the use of violence to achieve these goals. The JBAKC's basic premise is that the Ku Klux Klan is a paramilitary branch of the American government, a premise that considerably expands the meaning of [its] slogan "Death to the Klan."*[26]

Revolutionary Fighting Group, The Armed Resistance Unit, The United Freedom Front, The Red Guerrilla Resistance. Officials believe that most members of these white revolutionary groups committed to secretly banding together to fight what they believe is American imperialism are now in jail. During 1984–85, these groups claimed responsibility for bombs that exploded in buildings in New York City and Washington, D.C., including the IBM and Motorola offices, and the Senate wing of the U.S. Capitol, which was not in session at the time.

FALN—Puerto Rican National Liberation Armed Forces. Considered one of the most active U.S. terrorist groups, FALN demands Puerto Rican independence and claims responsibility for several terrorist acts, including bombings. With perhaps fewer than a dozen members, and most of them now jailed, FALN continues to operate in cooperation with other incarcerated groups such as NAPO and the Black Liberation Army. "Between 1974 and 1985, the group was responsible for nearly 150 bombings and incendiary attacks."[27] On June 19, 1988, the *New York Times* reported that a federal grand jury was still investigating FALN, trying to link it to scores of unsolved bombings around the nation. In 1979, leader William Morales escaped from custody, reportedly with the help of the Black Liberation Army and the May 19th Communist Organization. He is still at large.

Omega 7. Omega 7 consists of a small band of Cuban exiles in America that is committed to overthrowing President Fidel Castro of Cuba. Its leader, Eduardo Arocena, is in prison for murder, bombings, and other terrorist activities.

←　　→

For most of these groups, the U.S. government is the imperialist enemy, and prisoners are considered "prisoners of war." Although responsible for scattered bombings, left-wing groups for the most part have been minimally active in recent years, probably because most leaders and the more violent members are now in jail. All the groups actively recruit new members. And as imprisoned members of the various extremist groups are released over the next decade, their potential for violence will continue.

CHAPTER ELEVEN

FIGHTING EXTREMISM

The Rights of Extremists. Free speech is one of the most significant rights granted to all Americans by the Constitution. A free society cannot exist if only certain viewpoints are allowed. The price we pay for the freedom to speak our minds is having to tolerate other people's ideas, no matter how ugly and hateful. Although the mean-spirited, malicious slogans and philosophy of many American extremists are undemocratic, the Bill of Rights of the U.S. Constitution protects the rights of any minority to speak its mind.

But what about extremist groups such as neo-Nazis, that admit that if they were to succeed in obtaining power, they would curb free speech? Even then, the American Civil Liberties Union (ACLU)—the nation's most prominent organization dedicated to protecting the rights of minorities and individuals—claims that Nazis have the right to express themselves. Although the ACLU does not support the Nazis' views (in fact, most members would admit to loathing their ideas), it does defend "everyone's right to speak or demonstrate peacefully, without regard to the views of the person or groups involved. The organization's philosophy holds that unpopular groups are especially in need of protection under the Bill of Rights."[1]

In reaction to the vicious racist slurs by white supremacists and other racial and religious bigots, some scholars have pushed for outlawing such racist slander. But . . .

> *Prohibiting hate speech goes against the American grain. The Constitution is rooted in Enlightenment notions of pluralism and tolerance. The American consensus . . . is that even the most hateful opinions should be allowed to compete in the "marketplace" of ideas. And as a nation made up of minorities, we are loath to let the majority silence any faction, no matter how divisive or offensive.*[2]

Some speech, however, *is* outlawed. The U.S. Supreme Court has ruled that obscenity, libel, "fighting words" that are likely to cause violence, and giving away government secrets are unlawful. Some experts want racist rhetoric that could incite violence to be added to that list. Liberal democracies such as England, Israel, and much of Western Europe outlaw such speech. Should we? First Amendment scholars say no. If we ban one kind of speech, it might suppress other forms of valid, though unpopular forms of expression. Outlawing such speech would give courts the power to decide what's lawful speech and what's not; this power could be abused, experts fear, and eventually be used to suppress even more types of free expression:

> *As First Amendment lawyer Floyd Abrams argued " . . . Americans have made a brave and sophisticated choice," deciding to endure some hateful speech in the interest of a greater good: robust political debate.*[3]

If we aren't going to outlaw what extremists say, how can we guard against the effects of their undemocratic and violence-prone philosophies?

Curbing Extremism. Although what extremists *say* shouldn't be outlawed in a free democracy, what extremists *do* can be. In the past decade, several old laws have been more strictly enforced while some new laws have prohibited certain acts and stiffened the penalties for committing these acts.

Enforcing Laws. When extremists travel or communicate over state lines to plan or commit violence, the U.S. Justice Department can prosecute them under federal civil rights laws. Federal officials have also prosecuted some lawless extremists in recent years by using a racketeering and corrupt-organizations law. Laws that prohibit defacement of property and harassment have also been more rigidly enforced to fight extremist acts.

Extremism has also been combatted in recent years by new interpretations of old laws. One important precedent was set in 1987 when the Supreme

Court decided in favor of a Maryland synagogue that had been defaced by anti-Jewish graffiti. The Court maintained that the temple could receive financial damages under the 1866 civil rights law prohibiting discrimination based on race. As a result, vandalized institutions may now more easily sue for civil damages, or monetary rewards, and extremist groups are penalized where it hurts the most: in the pocketbook.

Similarly, when the mother of the lynched Michael Donald won $7 million in damages from the Ku Klux Klan for violating her son's civil rights (see Chapter One), an important precedent was set. Not only were the individuals who killed Donald sent to prison for their criminal acts, but their organization was held responsible for their behavior because the killers were acting on behalf of their organization. Forcing organizations to pay large financial damages to victims not only helps compensate the victims for their suffering, but it also discourages groups from inciting violence and helps to financially cripple organizations that foster violent crimes.

New Laws. Recently, twenty-nine states have adopted laws against religious vandalism, increasing the penalties for such crimes when the acts are motivated by discrimination toward race, religion, or nationality of the victim. Such laws crack down hard, for example, on cross-burnings and painting swastikas on synagogues. Several states and communities have also adopted antiviolence laws and have prohibited a convicted felon from having a weapon.

One of the most successful new laws that curb today's extremist groups has been the outlawing of paramilitary training. This law has been adopted so far in eighteen states: Arkansas, California, Colorado, Connecticut, Florida, Georgia, Idaho, Illinois, Michigan, Missouri, Nebraska, New Jersey, North Carolina, Oregon, Pennsylvania, Rhode Island, Virginia, and West Virginia. In the early 1980s, the Anti-Defamation League (ADL) of B'nai B'rith reported that numerous secret camps were offering instruction in handling weapons, knife fighting, guerrilla warfare, and so on. Since these laws have been enacted, the ADL reports that such activities have been halted. Whether these laws have driven such training camps further underground, to other states, or, in fact, have successfully suppressed such instruction is not known.

Other relevant laws that have been adopted in some states and communities include:

Banning masks or hoods in public unless for Halloween or other holidays

Prohibiting harassment and intimidation

Outlawing all weapons at marches and parades

Prohibiting cross-burnings when used for intimidation

As law enforcement officials have increasingly recognized that "militant racists are essentially domestic terrorists who present a real threat to society,"[4] more members of organized hate groups have been indicted in the 1980s than ever before. These laws and others have allowed federal officials to undertake "the most sweeping crackdown on the far right in the United States since World War II."[5]

To keep close track of extremists and their violent acts, more than half a dozen states now require the police to keep official records of hate crimes, and the House of Representatives passed a bill in 1987 that requires the collection of hate-crime statistics on a national level. Such monitoring helps to identify trends and to track extremists and their activities.

Changing Attitudes. As towns suffer job losses or community problems over racial issues, extremist groups often go there to offer support and incite emotions over the racial issues. What can individuals do to combat the hate messages these groups bring to town?

> *The greatest allies hate groups have in a community are fear and silence, and the greatest enemy is simple, unequivocal, public rejection.*[6]

Silence, passivity, and denial will only allow hate groups to fester, to grow, and to infect our society. To fight extremists and their violent acts, public statements must be made that reject racial and religious slurs and hate.

As more people understand how frustration and anger can lead to scapegoating and prejudice, they will be less apt to blame an entire race or religion for their problems. When such people encounter blatant racism, it is their responsibility to counteract it by acknowledging and identifying the problem, educating others, resisting the extremist groups, and providing real alternatives for those who might be particularly susceptible to the extremists' rhetoric. To ignore racism is to encourage it to snowball:

History has clearly shown the danger of ignoring such racism. The horror of Nazi Germany's holocaust against Jews is but the most extreme and familiar example. So even though the Klan and other groups like them are a tiny minority in the United States, they must be taken seriously, and the roots of the racism that perpetuates them must be understood.[7]

CHAPTER TWELVE

THE OUTLOOK FOR EXTREMISM

In spite of a record number of convictions against members of extremist groups and new laws that crack down hard on racial harassment, paramilitary training, and violations of civil rights, the danger of extremism in America today still lurks.

Whether left or right wing, extremism too often means terrorism. Both left- and right-wing groups have stockpiled weapons and committed robberies, bombings, and murders. Both right-wing extremists (primarily bigots and white supremacists) and left-wing extremists (primarily black separatists or revolutionaries) seek to cripple the U.S. government and to replace it with their own brand of authoritarian rule:

Both [rightists and leftists] are elitists who claim a monopoly of truth and the right to forcibly impose it on the majority. Both view the ordinary American citizen with contempt. And both seek to replace the American democratic system with a form of totalitarianism.[1]

Just because Klan membership is dwindling and most leaders of the far right and far left are in prison doesn't mean the threat has subsided. "The danger of violence rises, in the view of some authorities on extremist movements, not when their [the extremists'] hopes and numbers swell but when they shrink, and frustration explodes."[2]

Furthermore, some of the most powerful right-wing white supremacist leaders, though aging and ailing, are still free and actively forging alliances with other diverse far-right groups. As like-minded extremists band together, their movement is strengthened, and the threat to society looms ever larger.

The immediate dangers posed by extremist groups today are their terrorist acts and the racism and anti-Semitism they espouse. Though their memberships may be small, their influence is powerful. The far-reaching effect of today's extremism is that as their ugly ideas become ever more visible, hate and violence-prone racism could become increasingly commonplace and socially acceptable.

In the meantime, as more Vietnamese, Cambodian, Hispanic, and other recent immigrants to the United States find jobs and homes and as their children get into good colleges, some whites feel their security and power base slipping.[Some Americans believe that the gains of blacks and immigrants are at their own expense threatening their welfare.] The result is escalating resentment that is all too often vented through violence. And that is just what is happening: "Acts of violence against racial and ethnic groups, and against homosexuals, have reached epidemic proportions across the United States. . . ."[3]

"Bigoted violence" jumped from 99 incidents in 1980 to 276 in 1986, according to the Justice Department.[4] During those years, almost three thousand violent acts incited by racism were committed, reported the Center for Democratic Renewal.[5] And, increasingly, individuals rather than organized hate groups have committed the violence, which implies that "the phenomenon [is] diffusing into the general population."[6]

Similarly, violent acts against Jews jumped from 49 in 1979 to 638 in 1985.[7] By 1988, they soared to 1,281—a 26 percent jump from 1987.[8] Of those arrested in 1988 for anti-Semitic acts, 90 percent were under the age of twenty-one.[9] In addition, the Harris Poll reported in 1986 that 30 percent of Americans felt that Jews were more interested in money than in people and that some 25 percent to 30 percent of the American population were actively anti-Semitic.[10]

Equally troubling has been the surge of racism on college campuses where society usually sees its most liberal element and where much of the civil rights support was generated in the 1950s and 1960s:

Two decades after the Love Generation traded in its tribal beads for briefcases and business suits, bigotry and prejudice are making a comeback. Underlying this ugly renaissance is a change in the nation's political climate from the idealism that spawned the civil rights movements in the 1960s to the me-first ethic that has flourished in the '80s.[11]

The Center for Democratic Renewal reported a four-fold increase in collegiate racial incidents between 1985 and 1987, up from 14 in 1985 to 56 in 1987.[12] Some 174 colleges have experienced such violence on their campuses, including the University of California at Berkeley, Stanford University, Smith College in Massachusetts, Yale,[13] Temple University in Philadel-

phia, Indiana University, the University of Texas, Columbia University, Purdue University, Johns Hopkins University, and the University of Michigan.[14]

One primary reason for the wave of racial tension at colleges is that as the competition for college admittance, jobs, and promotions grows keener, students are more apt to protect their own positions and to emphasize their own identities.

UCLA Vice-Chancellor Winston Doby in a December 1988 issue of *College Woman* stated:

In the '60s, there were huge issues on campus which united students. Vietnam. Civil rights. Today, nothing produces that transcendence over differences. So we get student groups of different ethnic backgrounds competing— for space, for limited student funds. When decisions go against them, they sometimes believe the reasons are ethnic, racial. They firm up their identities within groups, and put other groups down.

A new surge of racism and bigotry has been found on America's college campuses, usually regarded as places of enlightened thought. People like Allan Vincent, a Nazi leader, seen here at San Francisco State College, have appeared more frequently on college campuses.

For many of today's youth, the civil rights movement is ancient history. Oblivious to the struggle for racial equality, many take the social gains for granted; some challenge whether we've done too much for minorities. A major criticism of the Reagan administration was that it largely ignored minority concerns and civil rights. During Reagan's eight years, opponents of affirmative action programs became increasingly verbal, and racism sometimes became increasingly acceptable and even "politically fashionable."[15]

At the same time, America is embracing an increasingly militaristic stance in its culture. The movie *Rambo*, for example, broke film records; *Rambo: Part II First Blood* grossed more than $75 million in less than four weeks. War toy sales have mushroomed to a billion-dollar industry, jumping more than 600 percent in sales between 1982 and 1986. The average American child is exposed to some 250 war cartoons and 800 TV commercials for war toys annually.[16]

Moreover, Americans are losing faith in the ability of the police to protect them:

> *Responsible, law-abiding citizens—afflicted by a lack of confidence in the police, reading every morning and watching on TV every night the stories about shootouts endangering innocent bystanders—[have] start[ed] arming themselves in case they have to join the battle.*[17]

Half of all American households—about 50 million to 60 million—own at least one gun.[18] Experts estimate that as many as 600,000 machine guns are at large, outside the military.[19] Weekend war games, where individuals engage in a simulated "war," are being played over more than six hundred fields across the country. More than half a million Americans subscribe to survival or paramilitary magazines that are full of articles on survivalism, weapon use, and guerrilla tactics.

Meanwhile, paranoia is growing as the budget deficit skyrockets, the AIDS epidemic threatens our health and health-care system, the farm belt struggles with surviving, our economic position slips worldwide as the trade deficit grows larger, and tensions peak about international relations. Such times can cause fear, insecurity, frustration, and anger, which, in turn, inflame scapegoating and racial stereotyping. The result has been a "resurgence of racism."[20]

"Frightened and increasingly mean-spirited people perpetuate the blight of racism everywhere, from the boroughs of New York to the backwaters of the Deep South,"[21] warns journalist James Coates. In such an environment, the threat of extremist groups goes beyond their scattered acts of terrorist violence.

The real threat of extremism in America is that intolerance will become more tolerated; that prejudice will become more politically and socially acceptable; that violence will increasingly be used as extremists try to obtain or reestablish their power and political control over the nation.

Although the right of free speech requires Americans to allow extremists to express their views, those views must not undermine the nation's democratic principles. While toleration of diverse opinions forms the essence of a free society, vigilance is the re-

sponsibility of all who value that freedom. If the goal of a democratic society is a more equitable, just, and free life, then the silence and passivity that allow hatred, racism, and bigotry to grow can become a cancer that poses a severe threat to the longest-living democracy the world has ever known: the United States of America.⌋

In the final analysis, one can frankly acknowledge that hate is taught. If each new generation were more tolerant of those who were different, perhaps hatred and prejudice, bigotry and resentment would someday disappear from our world.

SOURCE NOTES

Chapter One

1. Kornbluth, Jesse. "The Woman Who Beat the Klan," *New York Times Magazine*, November 1, 1987, p. 26.
2. Ibid.
3. Wade, Wyn Craig. *The Fiery Cross: The Ku Klux Klan in America* (New York: Simon & Schuster, 1987), p. 386.
4. Kornbluth, "The Woman Who Beat the Klan," p. 26.
5. Coates, James. *Armed and Dangerous: The Rise of the Survivalist Right* (New York: Hill & Wang, 1987), p. 7.
6. Ibid., pp. 7–8.
7. Ibid., p. 67.
8. Anti-Defamation League of B'nai B'rith, *Young and Violent: The Growing Menace of America's Neo-Nazi Skinheads* (New York, 1988), p. 11; and Center for Democratic Renewal, *Skinhead Nazis and Youth Information Packet* (Atlanta, 1988), p. 2.

Chapter Two

1. Allport, Gordon W. *The Nature of Prejudice* (Boston: Beacon Press, 1954), p. 247.
2. Archer, Jules. *The Extremists: Gadflies of American Society* (New York: Hawthorne Books, 1969), p. 99.

3. Curry, Richard O., John G. Sproat, and Kenyon C. Cramer, *The Shaping of America* (New York: Holt, Rinehart & Winston, 1972), p. 648.
4. Allport, *The Nature of Prejudice*, p. 7.
5. Daniels, Roger, and Harry H. L. Kitano. *American Racism: Exploration of the Nature of Prejudice* (Englewood Cliffs, N.J.: Prentice Hall, 1970), p. 9.
6. Moore, William V. *Extremism in the United States: A Teaching Resource Focusing on Neo-Nazism* (National Education Association, 1983), p. 15.
7. Rubenstein, Richard. *Alchemists of Revolution: Terrorism in the Modern World* (New York: Basic Books, 1987), p. 128.
8. Lipset, Seymour Martin, and Earl Raab. *The Politics of Unreason: Right-Wing Extremism in America, 1790–1970.* (New York: Harper & Row, 1970).
9. Bouchier, David. *Radical Citizenship: The New American Activism* (New York: Schocken Books, 1987), p. 10.
10. Ibid.
11. Ibid., p. 18.
12. Allport, *The Nature of Prejudice*, p. 349.
13. Ibid., p. 364.
14. L. Lowenthal, and N. Guterman. *Prophets of Deceit: A Study of the Techniques of the American Agitator* (New York: Harper, 1949); in Allport, pp. 414–15.

Chapter Three

1. Southern Poverty Law Center. *The Ku Klux Klan: A History of Racism and Violence* (Montgomery, Ala: Klanwatch, 1988), p. 24.
2. Archer, Jules. *The Extremists: Gadflies of American Society* (New York: Hawthorne Books, 1969), p. 99.
3. Ibid., p. 100.
4. Anti-Defamation League of B'nai B'rith. *Hate Groups in America: A Record of Bigotry and Violence.* (New York, 1988), p. 75.
5. Southern Poverty Law Center, *The Ku Klux Klan*, p. 25.
6. Coates, James. *Armed and Dangerous: The Rise of the Survivalist Right* (New York: Hill & Wang, 1987), p. 33.
7. Southern Poverty Law Center, *The Ku Klux Klan*, p. 15.
8. Meltzer, Milton. *The Truth about the Ku Klux Klan* (New York: Franklin Watts, 1982), p. 47.
9. Anti-Defamation League, *Hate Groups in America*, p. 81.
10. Southern Poverty Law Center, *The Ku Klux Klan*, p. 21.

11. Anti-Defamation League of B'nai B'rith. *Extremism on the Right: A Handbook* (New York, 1988), p. 26.
12. Southern Poverty Law Center, *The Ku Klux Klan*, p. 31.
13. Anti-Defamation League, *Hate Groups in America*, pp. 17–18.
14. Wade, Wyn Craig. *The Fiery Cross: The Ku Klux Klan in America* (New York: Simon & Schuster, 1987), p. 368.
15. Anti-Defamation League, *Extremism on the Right*, p. 41.
16. Southern Poverty Law Center, *The Ku Klux Klan*, p. 34.
17. Ibid., p. 44.
18. Anti-Defamation League, *Extremism on the Right*, p. 133.
19. Ruffin, Jane, "Miller Given 5 Years in Jail for War Threats," *News and Observer*, (Raleigh, No. Carolina), January 5, 1988.
20. Starr, Mark, "Violence on the Right," *Newsweek*, March 4, 1985, p. 25.
21. Southern Poverty Law Center, *The Ku Klux Klan*, p. 45.

Chapter Four

1. Wade, Wyn Craig. *The Fiery Cross: The Ku Klux Klan in America* (New York: Simon & Schuster, 1987), p. 373.
2. Allport, Gordon W. *The Nature of Prejudice* (Boston: Beacon Press, 1954), p. 447.
3. Coates, James. *Armed and Dangerous: The Rise of the Survivalist Right* (New York: Hill & Wang, 1987), p. 100.
4. Smith, Carol J., "Rural Radical Right: Politics of Fear and Hatred amidst the Farm Crisis," in General Board of Church and Society, *New Era of Hate*, (Washington, D.C.: June 1987), p. 22.
5. Center for Democratic Renewal. *Aryan Nations Far Right Underground Movement* (*Charlotte Observer*, July 26, 1986), p. 16.
6. Coates, *Armed and Dangerous*, p. 81.
7. National Public Radio, "All Things Considered," Nov. 21, 1988.
8. Zeskind, Leonard. *The "Christian Identity" Movement: Analyzing Its Theological Rationalization for Racist and Anti-Semitic Violence* (Atlanta: Division of Church and Society of the National Council of the Churches of Christ in the USA, 1986), p. 7.
9. Coates, *Armed and Dangerous*, p. 103.

Chapter Five

1. National Public Radio, "All Things Considered," November 21, 1988.

2. Winchester, Simon, "Idaho's Half-Baked Messiah," *Present Tense*, May–June 1987, p. 8.
3. Wade, Wyn Craig. *The Fiery Cross: The Ku Klux Klan in America* (New York: Simon & Schuster, 1987), p. 400.
4. Starr, Mark, "Violence on the Right," *Newsweek*, March 4, 1985, p. 26.
5. Bishop, Katherine, "Judging the Danger on the Right Fringe," *New York Times*, "Week in Review," March 6, 1988, p. 5.
6. Egan, Timothy, "Warriors of Hate Find No Homeland in Idaho," *New York Times*, January 2, 1988, p. 9.
7. Lindsay, Sue, "Order Wanted to Kill Jews, Witness Says," *Rocky Mountain News*, November 3, 1987.
8. Coates, James. *Armed and Dangerous: The Rise of the Survivalist Right* (New York: Hill & Wang, 1987), p. 43.
9. Center for Democratic Renewal. *Racist and Far-Right Organizing in the Pacific Northwest* (Atlanta, 1988), p. 3.
10. Anti-Defamation League of B'nai B'rith. *Hate Groups in America: A Record of Bigotry and Violence* (New York, 1988), p. 42.
11. "Acquittal of the Haters," *Time*, April 18, 1988, p. 33.
12. Dorsey, Frank, "Who Is the Villain? The Posse Knows!" in General Board of Church and Society, *New Era of Hate*, (Washington, D.C., June 1987), p. 24.
13. Bennett, David. *The Party of Fear: From Nativist Movements to the New Right in American History* (Chapel Hill: University of North Carolina Press, 1988), p. 355.
14. Coates, *Armed and Dangerous*, p. 118.
15. Bennett, *The Party of Fear*, p. 352.
16. Coates, *Armed and Dangerous*, p. 111.
17. Anti-Defamation League of B'nai B'rith, "William Pierce and the Neo-Nazi Church," *Special Edition*, February 1987.
18. Coates, *Armed and Dangerous*, p. 144.
19. Ostling, Richard N., "A Sinister Search for Identity," *Time*, October 20, 1986, p. 74.
20. Anti-Defamation League of B'nai B'rith. *Extremism on the Right: A Handbook* (New York, 1988), pp. 14, 58; and Anti-Defamation League, *Hate Groups in America*, pp. 44–46.

Chapter Six

1. Anti-Defamation League of B'nai B'rith. *Hate Groups in America: A Record of Bigotry and Violence* (New York, 1988), p. 24.
2. Coplon, Jeff, "Skinhead Nation," *Rolling Stone*, December 1, 1988, p. 56.

3. Center for Democratic Renewal, "Far-Right Youth Recruitment," *The Monitor*, September 1987, *Skinhead Nazis and Youth Information Packet* (Atlanta, 1988), p. 4.
4. Bishop, Katherine, "Judging the Danger on the Right Fringe," *New York Times*, March 16, 1988, p. 5; and Southern Poverty Law Center, *History of the KKK*, p. 55.
5. Anti-Defamation League of B'nai B'rith. *Young and Violent: The Growing Menace of America's Neo-Nazi Skinheads* (New York, 1988), p. 4.
6. Coplon, Jeff, "Skinhead Nation," p. 56.
7. Berry, Jason, "Goodbye, Klan; Hello, G.O.P.," *New York Times*, February 13, 1989, p. A21.
8. Coplon, "Skinhead Nation," p. 62.
9. Siemaszko, Corky, "Skinheads: Rebels without Cause," *Tampa Tribune*, April 17, 1988.
10. King, Wayne, "Violent Racism Attracts New Breed: Skinheads, *New York Times*, January 1, 1989, p. 35.
11. Siemaszko, Corky, "Skinheads: Rebels Without Cause. . . ," *Tampa Tribune*, April 17, 1988.
12. Center for Democratic Renewal, "Nazi Youth Gangs Inspire Alarm," *The Monitor*, June 1986, in *Skinhead Nazis and Youth Information Packet*.
13. Zimmerman, Ann, "Neo-Nazis on the move to voice a battle cry of white supremacy, *Dallas Times Herald*, April 17, 1988.
14. National Public Radio, "All Things Considered," Nov. 21, 1988.
15. Anti-Defamation League, *Young and Violent*, p. 11.
16. All racial incidents mentioned thus far are from the Anti-Defamation League's *Young and Violent* special report.

Chapter Seven

1. Suall, Irwin, and David Lowe, "The Hate Movement Today: A Chronicle of Violence and Disarray," *Terrorism*, Vol. 10, No. 4, 1987, p. 361.
2. Morlin, Bill, "Butler Welcomes Skinheads into Aryan World Congress," *Spokesman-Review* (Spokane, Washington), July 16, 1988.
3. National Public Radio, "All Things Considered," Nov. 21, 1988.
4. Anti-Defamation League of B'nai B'rith. *Young and Violent: The Growing Menace of America's Neo-Nazi Skinheads* (New York, 1988), p. 9.
5. Applenoum, Peter, "New Report Warns of Alliance of Racist Groups," *New York Times*, February 6, 1989.

6. Anti-Defamation League, *Young and Violent*, p. 29.
7. Rosenblatt, Roger, *Time*, October 21, 1985, p. 102.
8. Anti-Defamation League of B'nai B'rith, "Electronic Hate," *Special Edition*, July 1987.
9. Bates, Warren, "Police Watching Radical Group," *Las Vegas Review Journal*, April 25, 1988.
10. Anti-Defamation League of B'nai B'rith, "Louis Farrakhan," *Special Edition*, October 1987.

Chapter Eight

1. Southern Poverty Law Center. *The Ku Klux Klan: A History of Racism and Violence* (Montgomery, Ala.: Klanwatch, 1988), p. 32.
2. Winchester, Simon, "Idaho's Half-Baked Messiah," *Present Tense*, May–June 1987, p. 10.
3. Anti-Defamation League of B'nai B'rith, "Electronic Hate," *Special Edition*, July 1987.
4. Ibid.
5. Lowe, David, "Computerized Networks of Hate," *USA Today*, July 1985, p. 10.
6. Coates, James. *Armed and Dangerous: The Rise of the Survivalist Right* (New York: Hill & Wang, 1987), p. 194.
7. Anti-Defamation League of B'nai B'rith. *Hate Groups in America: A Record of Bigotry and Violence* (New York, 1988), p. 21.
8. Ibid., p. 21.
9. Henderson, Bruce, "White Racists Exploit Youthful Fervor," *Charlotte Observer*, October 7, 1987.
10. Lapin, Lisa, "White Supremacists Win Teen Converts," *San Jose Mercury News*, April 19, 1987.
11. Suall, Irwin, "Extremist Groups Seek Recruits in Prisons," *USA Today*, September 1987, p. 23.
12. Moore, William V. *Extremism in the United States: A Teaching Resource Focusing on Neo-Nazism* (National Education Association, 1983), p. 18.
13. Ibid., p. 97.

Chapter Nine

1. Anti-Defamation League of B'nai B'rith, "The Liberty Lobby Network," *Special Edition*, October 1987,

2. Anti-Defamation League of B'nai B'rith. *Extremism on the Right: A Handbook* (New York, 1988), p. 74.
3. Ibid., p. 74.
4. Ibid., p. 55.
5. Center for Democratic Renewal, "Background Report on Racist and Far-Right Organizing in the Pacific Northwest," (Atlanta, 1988), p. 8.
6. Anti-Defamation League of B'nai B'rith, "The Populist Party: Politics of Right-Wing Extremism," *ADL Facts*, Fall 1985, p. 1.
7. Ibid., p. 2.
8. Ibid., p. 9.
9. Bennett, David. *The Party of Fear: From Nativist Movements to the New Right in American History* (Chapel Hill: University of North Carolina Press, 1988), p. 357.
10. King, Dennis. *Nazis Without Swastikas: The Lyndon LaRouche Cult and Its War on American Labor* (New York: League for Industrial Democracy, 1982), p. 7.
11. Coates, James. *Armed and Dangerous: The Rise of the Survivalist Right* (New York: Hill & Wang, 1987), p. 201.
12. King, *Nazis Without Swastikas*, p. 9.
13. Anti-Defamation League of B'nai B'rith, "The LaRouche Political Cult: Packaging Extremism," *ADL Special Report*, Spr 1986, p. 1.
14. Ibid., p. 1.
15. Coates, *Armed and Dangerous*, p. 203–04.
16. Gelman, David, "Lyndon LaRouche; Beyond the Fringe," *Newsweek*, April 7, 1986, p. 38.
17. Ibid.
18. Anti-Defamation League, "The LaRouche Political Cult," p. 40.

Chapter Ten

1. *New Statesman*, December 13, 1985.
2. *MacLean's*, January 20, 1986.
3. *New Statesman*, December 13, 1985.
4. *Time*, October 21, 1985.
5. *New Statesman*, December 13, 1985.
6. Ibid.
7. *Washington Post*, July 27, 1985.
8. *Los Angeles Times*, September 17, 1985.
9. *Miami Times*, September 13, 1984.
10. *New York* magazine, October 21, 1985.

11. *Time*, October 21, 1985.
12. *New Statesman*, op. cit.
13. *Ithaca Journal*, February 11, 1989.
14. *New Statesman*, op. cit.
15. *New York*, October 7, 1985.
16. *New Republic*, October 28, 1985.
17. *USA Today* (magazine), September 1987.
18. *Chicago Sun Times*, December 30, 1987.
19. Ibid.
20. Suall, Irwin, "Extremist Groups seek Recruits in Prisons," *USA Today*, September 1987, p. 23.
21. Ibid.
22. Ibid.
23. Ibid.
24. Anti-Defamation League of B'nai B'rith, "The John Brown Anti-Klan Committee," *Special Edition*, October 1986.
25. Ibid.
26. Ibid.
27. Raynor, Thomas. *Terrorism* (New York: Franklin Watts) 1987, p. 82.

Chapter Eleven

1. *U.S. News & World Report*, April 3, 1978, as quoted in William Moore, *Extremism in the United States* (National Education Association, 1983), p. 124.
2. Jacoby, Tamar, "Time To Outlaw Racial Slurs?" *Newsweek*, June 6, 1988, p. 59.
3. Ibid.
4. Southern Poverty Law Center. *The Ku Klux Klan: A History of Racism and Violence* (Montgomery: Klanwatch, 1988), p. 46.
5. Suall, Irwin, and David Lowe, "The Hate Movement Today: A Chronicle of Violence and Disarray," *Terrorism*, Vol. 10, No. 4, 1987, p. 345.
6. Southern Poverty Law Center, *The Ku Klux Klan*, p. 29.
7. Ibid., p. 27.

Chapter Twelve

1. Anti-Defamation League of B'nai B'rith. *"Propaganda of the Deed": The Far Right's Desperate 'Revolution'*, (New York: ADL 1985), p. 2.

2. Scigliano, Eric, "America's Down-Home Racists," *Nation*, August 30, 1986, p. 1.
3. *Christian Century*, February 3, 1988.
4. *U.S. News & World Report*, February 2, 1987.
5. *Christian Century*, February 3, 1988.
6. Walters, Ronald, "White Radical Nationalism in the United States," *Without Prejudice*, Vol. I, Fall 1987, p. 7.
7. Coates, James p. 260.
8. Graham, Renee, "34 Percent Rise Recorded in anti-Semitic Acts in Mass.," *Boston Globe*, January 27, 1989, p. 1.
9. AP, "US Anti-Semitic Incidents Reported at 5-year High," *Sarasota Herald Tribune*, January 27, 1989, p. 13A.
10. Coates, p. 198–9.
11. Tift, Susan, "Bigots in the Ivory Tower," *Time*, January 23, 1989, p. 56.
12. Johnson, Hayes, "Racism Still Smolders on Campus," *USA Today*, May 10, 1988, p. 1.
13. Fernandez, Elizabeth. "Racism Lives on in Colleges," *San Francisco Examiner*, November 13, 1988 and Bayh, Birch, "Let's Tear Off Their Hoods," *Newsweek*, April 17, 1989.
14. Johnson, Hayes. "Racism Still Smolders on Campus" *USA Today*, May 10, 1988.
15. Berry, Jason. "Goodbye, Klan; Hello, G.O.P." (editorial) *New York Times*, February 13, 1989.
16. Coates, p. 265.
17. Church, George J., "The Other Arms Race," *Time*, February 6, 1989, p. 23.
18. Ibid., p. 26.
19. Coates, p. 266.
20. op. cit., Walters, p. 8.
21. Coates, p. 268.

FOR FURTHER READING

Anti-Defamation League of B'nai B'rith. *Hate Groups in America: A Record of Bigotry and Violence*. New York: Anti-Defamation League, 1988.

———, *Young and Violent: The Growing Menace of America's Neo-Nazi Skinheads*. New York: Anti-Defamation League, 1988.

Coates, James. *Armed and Dangerous: The Rise of the Survivalist Right*. New York: Hill & Wang, 1987.

Coplon, Jeff. "Skinhead Nation," *Rolling Stone*, December 1, 1988.

Herzstein, R. *The Nazis*. Englewood Cliffs, New Jersey: Messner, 1986.

Meltzer, Milton. *The Truth About the Ku Klux Klan*. New York: Franklin Watts, 1982.

Moore, Robert B. *Violence, the KKK and the Struggle for Equality*. New York: Council on Interracial Books for Children, Inc., 1981.

The National Institute Against Prejudice and Violence. *Striking Back at Bigotry: Remedies Under Federal and State Law for Violence Motivated by Racial, Religious and Ethnic Prejudice.* Baltimore, Maryland. [Discusses application of specific state and federal laws to hate crimes.]

Southern Poverty Law Center. *The Ku Klux Klan: A History of Racism and Violence.* Montgomery, Alabama: Klanwatch, 1988.

INDEX

Extremist groups (left-wing): and Louis Farrakhan, 128–34, *130;* miscellaneous groups of, 135–38
Extremist groups (nonviolent): and the Liberty Lobby, 117–18; and Lyndon LaRouche, 120–25, *123;* and the Populist Party, 118–20
Extremist groups (violent): computer networks use by, 111; group alliances of, *71,* 99–106, *102, 148;* media use by, *90,* 107–10, *109;* membership profile of, 115–16; prison recruitment by, 114–15; youth recruitment by, 80, 111, 113–15

Farrands, James, 49
Farrakhan, Louis, 105–6, 118, 128–34, *130*
Finger, Justin, 48
Freedom of speech, 139–41, 153

Harrell, John, 78, 79
Hispanics: and skinheads, 91, 95, 97; violence against, 97
Holocaust: as hoax, 58–59, 118; and Nazism, 33, *34,* 83, 118, 145
Homosexuals: and skinheads, 92, 95; violence against, 60

Identity Church, the: and the Aryan Nations, 66; and the Christian Defense League, 81; and the Order, 72; and The Posse Comitatus, 75; racism and, 58–63
Identity Mountain Church, 114

Immigrants: and Ku Klux Klan, 44; racism against, *19,* 24; and skinheads, 97; violence against, 45, 97
Innis, Roy, 90
Invisible Empire, the, 44, 49–50, 52

Jackson, Jesse, 129
Japanese-Americans, 21, 22
Jews: and the Aryan Nations, 67; and the Identity Church and, 58–59; and Lyndon LaRouche, 120–21; and the Order, 70; and The Posse Comitatus, 75; and skinheads, 91, 93, 95, 97; violence against, 45, 60, 70, 73, 97; and Zionist Occupational Government (ZOG), 59. *See also* Anti-Semitism
John Brown Anti-Klan Committee (JBAKC), 136

Kahl, Gordon, 75–77, 118
Kennedy, John F., 24
King, Coretta, 131
Klanwatch, 99
Klan Youth Corps, 111
Knights of the Ku Klux Klan, 49–50, 60
Know Nothings, 18, *19*
Koch, Ed, 133
Ku Klux Klan: and anti-Catholicism, 44; and anti-Semitism, 44, 53–55; and the Aryan Nations, 50, 66; and civil rights movement, 44; decline of, 46; and desegregation, 46; history of, 20, 40, *43;* and immigrants, 44; and Lyndon LaRouche, 120;

Paramilitary training: and the Aryan Nations, 69; and black separatism, 127; and CPDL, 78; and Ku Klux Klan, 52–53; laws against, 142–43; and Lyndon LaRouche, 120; and the Populist Party, 119

People Organized to Work for Economic Rebirth (POWER), 131

Pierce, William L., 86

Populist Party, the, 118–20

Posse Comitatus (power of the county), 67, 75–78, 115, 119

Powerlessness, 31–32

Prejudice, *154;* definition of, 23–25; extremism caused by, 29–32

Puerto Rican National Liberation Armed Forces (FALN), 137

Puritans, 18

Racism: and blacks, 11–12, 15–16, 20; and black separatism, 27, 105–6, 118, 127–34, *130,* 135; and Chinese, 21; on college campuses, 149–50, *150;* definition of, 23–25; and freedom of speech, 139–41; history of, 17–23, *19, 22;* and immigrants, 24; and Japanese-Americans, 21, *22;* and Jews, 13–15, 70; and Native Americans, 21; and the Populist Party, 118–20; and religious movement, 57–64, 65–81, *68, 79;* and skinheads, 95. *See also* Anti-Semitism; White supremacy; specific organizations

Radical leftists, 26

Red Guerrilla Resistance, the, 136–37

Religious movement causing racism, 57–64, 65–81, *68, 79*

Religious persecution, 18

Revolutionaries, 26

Revolutionary Fighting Group, 136–37

Right wing, 25–26

Right-wing extremism, 27, *123,* 147

Robb, Thom, 55, 59, *60*

Separatists, 27, 105–6, 118, 127–34, *130,* 135

Seymour, Doug, 93

Shelton, Robert, 48

Skinheads: and the Aryan Nations, 67, 103; and Ku Klux Klan, 49, 101, 103; and neo-Nazism, *71, 87,* 101; violence of, 15–16, 91–92, 94, *95,* 96–98

Southern National Front, 113

Southern Poverty Law Center, 39, 42, 48–52, *51,* 53, 56, 104

Stereotyping, 23–25

Students for a Democratic Society (SDS), 127

The United Freedom Front, 136–37

The United Klans of America (UKA), 48–49

Vigilantism, 27

Vincent, Allan, *150*

Wade, Wyn Craig, 67

Weather Underground, 127, 135